John Douglas Borthwick

Borthwick Castle

Or, sketches of Scottish history. With biographical notices of the chiefs of the house of Argyll

John Douglas Borthwick

Borthwick Castle

Or, sketches of Scottish history. With biographical notices of the chiefs of the house of Argyll

ISBN/EAN: 9783337012144

Printed in Europe, USA, Canada, Australia, Japan

Cover: Foto ©ninafisch / pixelio.de

More available books at **www.hansebooks.com**

BORTHWICK CASTLE;

OR

SKETCHES OF SCOTTISH HISTORY.

WITH

BIOGRAPHICAL NOTICES OF THE CHIEFS OF THE HOUSE OF ARGYLL.

BY

REV. J. DOUGLAS BORTHWICK,

AUTHOR OF

"Antonomasias of History and Geography," "Cyclopædia of History and Geography," "The British American Reader," "The Harp of Canaan," "Battles of the World," "Every Man's Mine of Useful Knowledge," "Elementary Geography of Canada," "History of Scottish Song," "Montreal its History and Biographical Sketches," and "Montreal its History and Commercial Register."

> "Loved country, when I muse upon
> Thy dauntless men of old
> Whose swords in battle foremost shone,
> Thy Wallace brave and bold,
> And Bruce, who for our liberty
> Did England's sway withstand;
> I glory I was born in thee,
> My own ennobled land."
>
> — Robert White.

"Qui Conducit."

MONTREAL:

Published by JOHN M. O'LOUGHLIN, Bookseller and Stationer
243 St. James St., of whom only, copies can be had.

1880

Printed by L. D. DUVERNAY proprietor of "Le Courrier de Montreal."

To
The Most Noble the Marquis of Lorne,
GOVERNOR GENERAL OF CANADA,

AND

Her Royal Highness the Princess Louise,

THIS VOLUME, ENTITLED,

"BORTHWICK CASTLE; OR, SKETCHES OF SCOTTISH HISTORY TO THE DEATH OF MARY,"

IS MOST RESPECTFULLY DEDICATED AND INSCRIBED, BY ONE WHO WELCOMES TO "THIS CANADA OF OURS" THE HEIR APPARENT OF ONE OF THE OLDEST AND MOST FAMOUS OF ALL CALEDONIA'S HISTORIC NAMES, WITH HIS

ILLUSTRIOUS CONSORT,

AND WHO — PRAYING ALMIGHTY GOD, LONG TO BLESS AND PROSPER THEM IN "HEALTH, WEALTH AND ESTATE,"— SUBSCRIBES HIMSELF THEIR MOST OBEDIENT AND HUMBLE SERVANT,

THE AUTHOR.

PREFACE.

THE Author publishes this little book with the fond hope that it may be found interesting to all lovers of Historical Research. He flatters himself that the arrangement is a better one than has ever before been given to the reading Public of Scottish Song and History; seeing that the most interesting points in the annals of the country as far down as it is carried—consist of both Prose and Poetry. When we consider the variety of extracts from such a galaxy of poetical minds as is found in the volume and all of them bearing on the subject of the book—the volume becomes doubly valuable. It is "multum in parvo"—a small library of History in one book. It will be prized too, as a Reader or Speaker amongst Scottish youth as some of the finest pieces of the English language are intermixed with his own prose history.

Perhaps one of the most interesting features of the work is the chapter which contains the Biographical Sketches of the House of Argyll. These sketches having been submitted for the approval of the present heir of the House of Campbell—our own Governor General—the Marquis of Lorne and H. R. H. the Princess Louise, and the Author having received their commendation that they were correct, feels that they will be read by thousands and that this is one of the valuable items of the work.

Trusting that the work will at least pay the cost—the Author launches it on the Public sea—feeling that the Vox Populi which has so favorably in years gone by stamped his other works will be extended to this, his last endeavour to cater to the Reading Public of Canada, and to stem, however feebly, the tide of the trashy and pernicious literature which nowadays is not only deluging the country but the minds of our rising sons and daughters—by giving them healthy patriotic and exciting historical sketches of a country which has produced a long list of heroes and heroines, and statesmen, and wonderful men of mind.

J. DOUGLAS BORTHWICK.

January 1880.

PROLOGUE.
ADDRESS TO SCOTLAND.

Oh, Scotia! by whatever name
The voice of history sounds thy fame;
From Artic clime to torrid strand,
Who has not heard of Scotia's land?
Land of my birth, whose rocks sublime
Defy, and scorn and spurn all time!
Land where the mountain and the wood,
From age to age unchanged have stood,
Despising tempest, torrent, sea—
Land of the brave, the fair, the free.
Thy children oft have fought and bled,
Nor grieved to see their life's-blood shed;
Whose war-cry in the hour of fight,
Was aye " St. Andrew and our right!"
Thy sons have fought in every land;
Their blood has dyed the Egyptian sand;
Up Abraham's heights they scaled their way,
And fought in Alma's bloody fray;
Have gained a never dying fame,
Immortal praise in Lucknow's name.
Unvanquished land, full many a foe
Has tried in vain to lay thee low;
In vain: thou hast thy freedom still—
Thou hast it now, and ever will.
Though other climes may boast the vine,
Whose tendrils round each cottage twine,
They cannot with thy mountains vie,
In all their rugged Majesty.
Though other shores are mild and fair
And breathe a spicy, balmy air,
They cannot give the bracing breeze
Within their bowers of sloth and ease.
No foreign land can vie with thee,
Unrivalled land of brave and free,
Thou land which ne'er shall be forgot,
Land of the Thistle and the Scot!

J. Douglas Borthwick.

BORTHWICK CASTLE;

OR

SKETCHES OF SCOTTISH HISTORY.

> Great Boadicea ———
> Thy very fall perpetuates thy fame,
> And Suetonius' laurels droop with shame,—"
>
> DIBDIN.

CHAPTER I.

Description of Scotland.—Arrival of the Romans under Julius Cæsar.—His Victory on the Kentish Shore.—Descriptions from the Commentaries.—Julius Agricola.—Boadicea.—The Druids.—Story of the Mistletoe: ("*Potter's American Monthly*.")

IT is now impossible even in this practical age of the world's history to find out, when Scotland was first inhabited, or when the ancient and primitive tribes first landed on its northern shores and spread themselves over its heather hills. There is nothing in all history — no written memorial or record of any kind whatever, to give us the information we are in search of — or to tell us who were or whither came the aboriginal inhabitants. Antiquity's darkest pall covers the whole subject, and it thus continues until the 55th year before the Christian Era,

In this ever memorable year — memorable to every British subject, in every part of our ever Gracious Majesty the Queen's vast dominions, and wherever the English language is spoken — the Romans, at this time the undisputable possessors and conquerors of almost the whole known world, made their first descent on the shores of Albion. Let the reader carry back his imagination to this important period. No modern writer can give so faithful and exact an account of this great expedition as he who was an eye-witness to and the commander of the whole. In the 4th Book of Cæsar's Commentaries, we have a graphic description of the landing of the Romans on the Kentish shore. In the 25th Chapter of that book, Cæsar thus writes: " Atque nostris militibus cunctantibus
" maxime propter altitudinem maris; qui X legio-
" nis aquilam ferebat, contestatus deos, ut ea res
" legioni feliciter eveniret: Desilite, inquit, com-
" militones, nisi vultis aquilam hostibus prodere,
" ergo, certé meum reipub. atque imperatori offici-
" um præstitero. Hoc quum magnâ voce dixisset,
" ex navi se projecit, atque in hostes aquilam ferre
" cœpit." " And whilst our men demurred (about
" venturing ashore) chiefly on account of the deep-
" ness of the sea, the standard-bearer of the tenth
" legion, imploring the gods that the thing might
" turn out lucky for the legion, Fellow-soldiers,
" said he, jump out, unless you have a mind to
" give up your eagle to the enemy. I, at least,
" shall perform my duty to the commonwealth and
" my general. Having said this with a loud voice,
" he leaped overboard, and began to advance the
" eagle towards the enemy."

This happened on a lovely afternoon of a beautiful day in September, when the leaves of the old oak trees in the English forests were beginning to be tinged with the glorious tints of an approaching autumnal season. Cæsar's fleet amounted to eighty ships of all sizes. The sturdy native Britons lined the beach, their army consisting of foot, horse, and chariots, and they opposed, with all their might, the landing of the Roman legions on their shores. Cæsar opened on the Islanders a heavy discharge— not of cannon balls and rifle bullets, for artillery was then unknown—but of stones and darts, from the Balista and Catapulta, warlike military engines which he had on board the fleet. This made the brave Britons retire a little, but after the 10th legion, Cæsar's favorite corps, with many others, amounting to 12,000 soldiers, entered the water, the Islanders were slowly driven back, and the Imperial army of Rome remained masters of the field. Thus for the first time, was the standard eagle of the conquering Romans planted on Albion's Isle.

Let us look for a moment to the Commentaries of the renowned Julius Cæsar, and give two additional extracts, relative to the occupation of Britain by the Romans,—he says :—

" The enemy being vanquished in battle, so
" soon as they recovered themselves after their
" flight, sent instantly to Cæsar to treat about a
" peace, and promised to give hostages, and submit
" to orders."

He then, in the 33rd Chapter describes graphically the ancient mode of fighting, by the inhabitants of Britain. " The manner of fighting from

"the chariots is this: in the first place they drive
"round to all quarters and cast darts, and with the
"very terror caused by their horses, and the rumb-
"ling noise of their wheels, they generally disorder
"the ranks, and having wrought themselves in
"betwixt the troops of the cavalry, they jump out
"of their chariots and fight on foot. Their drivers,
"in the meantime, retire a little from the action
"and so station the chariots, that in case they be
"overpowered by the enemies' numbers, they may
"have a free retreat to their friends. Thus in
"battles they act with the swiftness of cavalry
"and the firmness of infantry; and by daily expe-
"rience and practice become so expert, that they
"use on declining and sloping ground to check their
"horses at full gallop and quickly manage and turn
"them and run along the pole and rest on the
"harness and from thence, with great nimbleness,
"leap back into the chariots."

The Romans remained undisputed masters of all the southern parts of Great Britain, for one hundred and fifty years after Cæsar's victory on the Kentish shore. At this period the celebrated General Julius Agricola led his army across the border which then divided the conquered from the unconquered part of Britain, and began to hew and cut his way into the dense forest of Caledonia. After a great deal of hard fighting he at last, built a chain of strong forts between the firths of Clyde and Forth — but all the country to the north of these forts or what is called The Highlands of Scotland—could never be conquered or subdued; hence the Romans were in continual alarm and trouble from the incursions of these hardy Picts and Scots—which continued till the last legions of Rome left the Island — nearly four hundred years after Cæsar's victory at the Chalk Cliffs of Dover.

We cannot close this short account of the occupation by the Romans of Britain's Isle — without inserting the following poem of Cowper on this subject.

It is supposed that an ancient Druid is speaking to the British Queen and foretelling the greatness and the grandeur of that Empire upon which the sun never sets in his celestial circuit.

BOADICEA.

"When the Romans landed in Britain, Boadicea was queen of a tribe of Britons living on the eastern coast. Her husband, shortly before his death, had made a will dividing his property between his two daughters and the emperor of Rome; by which means he expected to make the Roman government friendly. But the plan entirely failed. After his death, his kingdom was plundered, and his family abused and maltreated in a most outrageous manner. Boadicea, rendered frantic by the injuries inflicted on herself and her daughters, gathered an army, and took the field against the Romans. Before the battle she rode along the ranks in a war chariot with her daughters behind her, and harangued the soldiers as she passed along the lines, denouncing the tyranny and the crimes of the Romans, and urging them to fight bravely in the coming conflict, and thus at once avenge her wrongs and save their common country. All, however, was vain. The battle was fiercely fought, but the Romans were victorious."

When the British warrior Queen,
    Bleeding from the Roman rods,
Sought, with an indignant mien,
    Counsel of her country's gods:

Sage beneath the spreading oak
    Sat the Druid, hoary chief;
Every burning word he spoke
    Full of rage and full of grief:—

"Princess! if our aged eyes
  Weep upon thy matchless wrongs,
'Tis because resentment ties
  All the terrors of our tongues.

"Rome shall perish!—write that word
  In the blood that she has spilt!
Perish, hopeless and abhorred,
  Deep in ruin as in guilt.

"Rome, for empire far renowned,
  Tramples on a thousand states;
Soon her pride shall kiss the ground—
  Hark! the Goth is at her gates!

"Other Romans shall arise,
  Heedless of a soldier's name;
Sounds, not arms, shall win the prize,
  Harmony the path to fame.

"Then the progeny that springs
  From the forests of our land,
Armed with thunder, clad with wings,
  Shall a wider world command.

"Regions Cæsar never knew
  Thy posterity shall sway;
Where his eagles never flew
  None invincible as they."

Such the bard's prophetic words,
  Pregnant with celestial fire,
Bending as he swept the chords
  Of his sweet but awful lyre.

> She, with all a monarch's pride,
>   Felt them in her bosom glow;
> Rushed to battle, fought, and died,—
>   Dying, hurled them at the foe:
>
> " Ruffians! pitiless as proud,
>   Heaven awards the vengeance due;
> Empire is on us bestowed,—
>   Shame and ruin wait for you!

At this period, all over France as well as Britain, prevailed that terrible and bloody religion which is known as the Druid. These Druids or men of the Oaks worshipped a supreme God or as he was styled —The Ruler of the World. They worshipped the sun also—under the name of Bel and made him the God of Medicine, because by his rays and heat—the healing plants and all the shrubs which they required in their arts and incantations were made to grow. They taught the doctrine of a future life but held like the Hindoos—that before the soul reached a state of happiness, it had to undergo a series of transmigrations, becoming the inhabitant of a succession of brute bodies. The oak tree was their sacred tree. Their places of worship were called Henges and their altars styled Kromlachs. They offered human victims in sacrifice. Plunging the sacrificial knive into the bosom of the poor wretch, they drew signs and omens from the manner in which it fell—the convulsions of the limbs and the spurting and flowing of the victim's blood. Sometimes they made huge wicker work figures of men filled them with human beings—afterwards burning both the figure and its contents to ashes. They pretended to cure all diseases—the grand remedy being a parasitic plant growing in the oak tree and called Mistletoe.

The power and influence of this singular order were immense. Whoever refused obedience to them was accursed and cut off from every right belonging to a human being. He was forbidden all use of fire and no man dared on pain of death to allow the poor shivering wretch to warm himself. All fled at his approach, lest they should be polluted by his touch. Such was the tremendous power which this giant superstition exercised over the brave but simple Caledonians or People of the woods, as well as over all the inhabitants of Britain.

Before concluding this first Chapter, it may be interesting to insert the following short article taken from a recent number of " Potter's American Monthly "—and which gives some items of useful information regarding the Mistletoe.

" This singular plant, so weirdly interwoven with the superstition and poetry of our Saxon forefathers, and inseparable from both heathen and Christian traditions of " Yule-tide," is a coarse, two-leaved evergreen growing on trees, as many of the mosses and fungi do. Its leaves are oblong, and between every pair of them is found a cluster of small, sticky berries—the same of which the substance called birdlime is made. During the Christmas week of 1872 the English " mistletoe bough " was offered for sale in Boston for the first time. We give our readers the following mythological account of this plant, still dear to every English home circle. The mistletoe was the holiest plant in nature to the

Druids and early Britons, for it represented their sun-god Hoius, of Eastern mythology (the offspring of Deo and Virgo, which the Egyptians represented by the Sphinx), as also Baldur, the loved and early lost, whose tale in the Norse mythology is like a sunshiny fragment of Ionian life, dropped into the stormy centre of Scandinavian existence. For Baldur, the holiest Druids sought with prayers and ceremonies on the sixth day of the moon the mistletoe which grew on the sacred oak. Its discovery was hailed with songs and sacrifices of white bulls. None but the chief priest might gather it, which was done by separating it from the tree with a golden knife. It was caught in the robe of a priest, and on no account allowed to touch the ground. In Denmark, Sweden and Norway, it has still names equivalent to " Baldur brow." It was in high reputation with all pretenders to the black art, and is authoritatively said to possess the power of resisting lightning. It grows in abundance in central Texas, and it is currently believed that even if the tree on which it grew were blasted by lightning, it was always uninjured. Chandler says that the custom of decking the house at Christmas with mistletoe is of pagan origin, and was done by the Druids to allure and comfort the sylvan spirits during the sleep of nature."

CHAPTER II.

CONTENTS:

St. Ninian, Palladius and St. Columba.—Duncan, King of Scotland.—Macbeth.—Extracts from Shakespeare.—Soliloquy of Macbeth.—Ditto.—Malcolm and Macduff in the English Court.—Macbeth on the death of his Queen.—Malcolm and Macduff after the Battle of Dunsinane.—William the Conqueror.—The Battle of Hastings by Charles Dickens.—Fugitives from England.—Edgar and his sister Margaret.—Malcolm marries Margaret.

"Only vaulting ambition which o'erleaps itself—
And fails on the other,"
MACBETH.

" A furious victor's partial will prevailed,
All prostrate lay; and in the secret shade,
Deep stung but fearful indignation gnashed his teeth—"
THOMSON.

IT is impossible to find out in what way Christianity was introduced into Scotland; but it is certain that the first great name with which this era is connected is that of St. Ninian, who is called by the " venerable Bede."—" The Apostle of the South of Scotland."—He founded a religious house or church at Whithorn in Wigtownshire and died in A. D. 432. Intimately connected with him was St. Patrick who went to Ireland, the year of St. Ninian's Death.—He died A. D. 460. In Scotland arose another great name Palladius who labored successfully among the Picts, to near the middle of the sixth century.—A well know disciple of his St. Kentigern or St. Mungo, established the faith among the Britons in the West.—St. Columba succeeded Palladius, but on account of the civil strifes of his country retired to Iona in A. D. 563 and founded the celebrated monastery there which became a centre of learning. From this time to the middle of the eighth century and on to that of the tenth, we know little of the Church in Scotland.

These names then of St. Ninian, Palladius and St. Columba are imperishably connected with the era succeeding that of the Druids. Druidical worship gave way before their kindly teachings. The long white-robed Druid priest neither cut the Mistletoe any more nor sacrificed the wretched victim on the Altar Stone.—The great circles of stones became deserted and in their place little churches began to be built all over the Island.

It continued thus until the reign of King Malcolm. This King is immortalized by Shakespeare, the renowned Bard of Avon—in his beautiful and well known Tragedy of Macbeth. Macbeth had murdered the previous King " Good King Duncan " and usurped the throne. Young Malcolm, his son, fled to England and lived for fifteen years at the English court, eating the bread and drinking the water of a lonely exile from his native land. At last, receiving help from the English King, he returned to Scotland, encountered Macbeth at Dunsinane and slew him. He thus ascended the Scottish throne and reigned in peace.

Some extracts from that immortal Tragedy must be inserted here as the " Play of Macbeth" tells us of one of the earliest periods in Scottish History. The exquisite morceaux which can be culled from this beautiful Tragedy are multitudinous, but space in this History, will enable us but to gather a few.

The terrible thoughts of Macbeth haunting his conscience previous to the murder of Duncan is one of the finest pieces of English composition.

" If it were done, when 'tis done, then 'twere well,
It were done quickly. If the assassination
Could trammel up the consequence, and catch,
With his surcease success; that but this blow
Might be the be-all and the end-all here,
But here upon this bank and shoal of time,
We'd jump the life to come. But in these cases
We still have judgment here;—that we but teach
Bloody instructions, which being taught, return
To plague the inventor. This even handed justice
Commends the ingredients of our poison'd chalice
To our own lips. He's here in double trust:
First, as I am his kinsman and his subject,
Strong both against the deed; then, as his host,
Who should against his murderer shut the door,
Not bear the knife myself. Besides, this Duncan
Hath borne his faculties so meek, hath been
So clear in his great office, that his virtues
Will plead like angels, trumpet-tongued, against
The deep damnation of his taking-off,
And pity, like a naked new-born babe,
Striding the blast, or heaven's cherubin hors'd
Upon the sightless couriers of the air,
Shall blow the horrid deed in every eye,
That tears shall drown the wind—I have no spur
To prick the sides of my intent, but only
Vaulting ambition, which o'er-leaps itself
And fails on the other."

These extracts would be incomplete without the well known soliloquy.

" Is this a dagger that I see before me ?
The handle toward my hand ? Come, let me clutch
                                                    thee ;—
I have thee not, and yet I see thee still
Art thou not, fatal vision ! sensible
To feeling, as to sight ? or art thou but
A dagger of the mind, a false creation
Proceeding from the heat oppressed brain ? .
I see thee yet, in form as palpable
As this which now I draw,
Thou marshal'st me the way that I was going;
And such an instrument I was to use,
Mine eyes are made the fools o' the other senses,
Or else worth all the rest,—I see thee still;
And on thy blade and dudgeon gouts of blood,
Which were not there before---There's no such thing;
It is the bloody business, which informs
Thus to mine eyes—Now o'er one half the world
Nature seems dead and wicked dreams abuse
The curtain'd sleep ; now witchcraft celebrates
Pale Hecate's offerings ; and wither'd murder
Alarm'd by his sentinel the wolf,
Whose howls' his watch, thus with his stealthy pace
With Tarquin's ravishing strides,towards his design
Moves like a ghost—Thou sure and firm set earth
Hear not my steps, which way they walk, for fear
The very stones watch of my whereabouts
And take the present horror from the time
Which now suits with it, —Whiles I threat he lives
Words to the heat of deeds too cold breath gives,
I go, and it is done ; the bell invites me,

Hear it not, Duncan ; for it is the knell
That summons thee to Heaven or Hell.

After the death of Duncan the scene changes to the court of the English King, where Rosse has brought news to Malcolm and Macduff of the massacre of the latter's whole family in Fife, by Macbeth, who is now to all appearance firmly seated on the Scottish throne. This sad event had been predicted by the tyrant himself where he says :

" The castle of Macduff I will surprise,
Seize upon Fife, give to the edge o' the sword
His wife, his babes, and all unfortunate souls
That trace his line.

After Rosse had brought the news Malcolm says to Macduff :

Be comforted,
Let's make us med'cines of our great revenge,
To cure this deadly grief.

Macduff.—He has no children—All my pretty ones?
Did you say all ? Oh Hell Kite ! All !
What, all my pretty chickens and their dam
At one fell swoop?

Malcolm.—Dispute it like a man.

Macduff.—I shall do so ;
But I must also feel it as a man,
I cannot but remember such things were,
That were most precious to me—did Heaven look on,
And would not take their part ? sinful Macduff,
They were all struck for thee ! naught that I am,

Not for their own demerits, but for mine,
Fell slaughter on their souls; Heaven rest them now!
Malcolm.—Be this the whetstone of your sword, let grief
Convert to anger, blunt not the heart, enrage it,
Macduff.—Oh! I could play the woman with mine eyes,
And braggart with my tongue! But gentle Heaven
Cut short all intermission; front to front,
Bring thou this fiend of Scotland and myself;
Within my sword's length set him; if he 'scape
Heaven forgive him too!
Malcolm.—This tune goes manly,
Come go we to the king, our power is ready;
Our lack is nothing but our leave, Macbeth
Is ripe for shaking, and the powers above
Put on their instruments, Receive what cheer you may;
The night is long, that never finds the day.

The well known words of Macbeth on the death of the Queen are familiar by every one.

" She should have died hereafter;
There would have been a time for such a word
To-morrow and to-morrow and to-morrow,
Creeps in this petty pace from day to day,
To the last syllable of recorded time;
And all our yesterdays, have lighted fools
The way to dusty death, out, out, brief candle
Life's but a walking shadow; a poor player,
That struts and frets his hour upon the stage

And then is heard no more: it is a tale
Told by an idiot, full of sound and fury,
Signifying nothing.

 Immediately after the Battle of Dunsinane Malcolm advanced all the Thanes who had fought for him to the rank of Earl the first time that this title was made in Scotland, Shakespeare says:

Macduff.—Hail, King! for so thou art. Behold
           where stand
 The usurper's cursed head, the time is free;
 I see thee compass'd with thy kingdom's pearl
 That speak my salutation in their minds;
 Whose voices I desire aloud with mine
 Hail! King of Scotland!
All.—King of Scotland, hail! (*flourish*)
Malcolm.—We shall not spend a large expense of
           time,
 Before we reckon with your several loves,
 And make us even with you. My thanes and
           kinsmen
 Henceforth be earls---the first that ever Scotland
 In such an honor nam'd. What's more to do,
 Which would be planted newly with the time
 As calling home our exil'd friends abroad,
 That fled the snares of watchful tyranny;
 Producing forth the cruel ministers
 Of this dead butcher and his fiend-like queen;
 Who, as 'tis thought, by self and violent hands
 Took off her life,—this and what needful else
 That calls upon us, by the grace of Grace,
 We will perform in measure time and place;
 So thanks to all at once—and to each one,
 Whom we invite to see us crown'd at Scone."

When Malcolm had been twelve years on the throne of Scotland, there came to the shores of England another invader like Julius Cæsar, William of Normandy by name. "The Conqueror" in English History. At the celebrated Battle of Hastings he attacked King Harold, and after a long and stout encounter the English King was slain and his army put to rout.

We must insert here the great English novelist's description of the Battle of Hastings; Charles Dickens very truthfully remarks that—

"HAROLD was crowned King of England on the very day of Edward the Confessor's funeral. When the news reached Norman William, hunting in his park at Rouen, he dropped his bow, returned to his palace, called his nobles to council, and presently sent ambassadors to Harold, calling on him to keep his oath, and resign the crown. Harold would do no such thing. The barons of France leagued together round Duke William for the invasion of England. Duke William promised freely to distribute English wealth and English lands among them. The Pope sent to Normandy a consecrated banner, and a ring containing a hair which he warranted to have grown on the head of St. Peter! He blessed the enterprise, and cursed Harold, and requested the Normans would pay "Peter's pence"—or a tax to himself of a penny a year on every house—a little more regularly in future, if they could make it convenient.

King Harold had a rebel brother in Flanders, who was a vassal of Harold Hardrada, king of Norway. This brother and this Norwegian king, joining their forces against England, with Duke William's help won a fight, in which the English were commanded by two nobles, and then besieged York. Harold, who was waiting for the Normans on the coast at Hastings, with his army, marched to Stamford bridge, upon the river Derwent, to give his brother and the Norwegians instant battle.

He found them drawn up in a hollow circle, marked out by their shining spears. Riding round this circle at a distance, to survey it, he saw a brave figure on horseback, in a blue mantle and a bright helmet, whose horse suddenly stumbled and threw him.

" Who is that man who has fallen ?" Harold asked of one of his captains.

" The King of Norway," he replied.

" He is a tall and stately king," said Harold, " but his end is near."

He added, in a little while, " Go yonder to my brother, and tell him if he withdraw his troops he shall be Earl of Northumberland, and rich and powerful in England."

The captain rode away and gave the message.

" What will he give to my friend the King of Norway?" asked the brother.

" Seven feet of earth for a grave," replied the captain.

" No more?" returned the brother with a smile.

" The King of Norway being a tall man, perhaps a little more," replied the captain.

" Ride back," said the brother, " and tell King Harold to make ready for the fight !"

He did so very soon. And such a fight King

Harold led against that force, that his brother, the Norwegian king, and every chief of note in all their host, except the Norwegian king's son, Olave, to whom he gave honourable dismissal, were left dead upon the field. The victorious army marched to York. As King Harold sat there at the feast, in the midst of all his company, a stir was heard at the doors, and messengers, all covered with mire from riding far and fast through broken ground, came hurrying in to report that the Normans had landed in England.

The intelligence was true. They had been tossed about by contrary winds, and some of their ships had been wrecked. A part of their own shore, to which they had been driven back, was strewn with Norman bodies. But they had once more made sail, led by the duke's own galley, a present from his wife, upon the prow whereof the figure of a golden boy stood pointing towards England. By day, the banner of the three lions of Normandy, the diverse coloured sails, the gilded vanes, the many decorations of this gorgeous ship, had glittered in the sun and sunny water; by night, a light had sparkled like a star at her mast head: and now, encamped near Hastings, with their leader lying in the old Roman castle of Pevensy, the English retiring in all directions, the land for miles around scorched and smoking, fired and pillaged, was the whole Norman power, hopeful and strong, on English ground.

Harold broke up the feast and hurried to London. Within a week, his army was ready. He sent out spies to ascertain the Norman strength. William took them, caused them to be led through his whole camp, and then dismissed. "The Normans," said these spies to Harold," are not bearded on the upper lip as we English are, but are shorn. They are priests." "My men," replied Harold, with a laugh, "will find those priests good soldiers."

"The Saxons," reported Duke William's outposts of Norman soldiers, who were instructed to retire as King Harold's army advanced, "rush on us through their pillaged country with the fury of madmen."

"Let them come, and come soon!" said Duke William.

Some proposals for a reconciliation were made, but were soon abandoned. In the middle of the month of October, in the year 1066, the Normans and the English came front to front. All night the armies lay encamped before each other, in a part of the country then called Senlac, now called (in remembrance of them) Battle. With the first dawn of day they arose. There, in the faint light, were the English on a hill; a wood behind them; in their midst the royal banner, representing a fighting warrior, woven in gold thread adorned with precious stones; beneath the banner, as it rustled in the wind, stood King Harold on foot, with two of his remaining brothers by his side; around them, still and silent as the dead, clustered the whole English army—every soldier covered by his shield, and bearing in his hand his dreaded English battleaxe.

On an opposite hill, in three lines—archers, footsoldiers, horsemen—was the Norman force. Of a sudden, a great battle-cry burst from the Norman lines. The English answered with their own battle-cry. The Normans then came sweeping down the hill to attack the English.

There was one tall Norman knight who rode before the Norman army on a prancing horse, throwing up his heavy sword and catching it, and singing of the bravery of his countrymen. An English knight who rode out from the English force to meet him, fell by this knight's hand. Another English knight rode out, and he fell too. But then a third rode out, and killed the Norman. This was in the beginning of the fight. It soon raged everywhere.

The English, keeping side by side in a great mass, cared no more for the showers of Norman arrows than if they had been showers of Norman rain. When the Norman horsemen rode against them, with their battle-axes they cut men and horses down. The Normans gave way. The English pressed forward. A cry went forth among the Norman troops that Duke William was killed. Duke William took off his helmet, in order that his face might be distinctly seen, and rode along the line before his men. This gave them courage. As they turned again to face the English, some of the Norman horse divided the pursuing body of the English from the rest, and thus all that foremost portion of the English fell, fighting bravely. The main body still remaining firm, heedless of the Norman arrows, and with their battle-axes cutting down the crowds of horsemen when they rode up, like forests of young trees, Duke William pretended to retreat. The eager English followed. The Norman army closed again, and fell upon them with great slaughter.

"Still," said Duke William, "there are thousands of the English, firm as rocks around their king. Shoot upward, Norman archers, that your arrows may fall down upon their faces."

The sun rose high, and sank, and the battle still raged. Through all that wild October day the clash and din resounded in the air. In the red sunset, and in the white moonlight, heaps upon heaps of dead men lay strewn, a dreadful spectacle, all over the ground. King Harold, wounded with an arrow in the eye, was nearly blind. His brothers were already killed. Twenty Norman knights, whose battered armour had flashed fiery and golden in the sunshine all day long, and now looked silvery in the moonlight, dashed forward to seize the royal banner from the English knights and soldiers, still faithfully collected round their blinded king. The king received a mortal wound, and dropped. The English broke and fled. The Normans rallied, and the day was lost.

Oh! what a sight beneath the moon and stars, when lights were shining in the tent of the victorious Duke William, which was pitched near the spot where Harold fell—and he and his knights were carousing within—and soldiers with torches, going slowly to and fro without, sought for the corpse of Harold among piles of dead—and the warrior, worked in golden thread and precious stones, lay low, all torn and soiled with blood—and the three Norman lions kept watch over the field!"

About two years after the Battle of Hastings some of the fugitives, escaping from their country, set sail for Scotland, and after a tedious and stormy voyage in their small ship, effected a landing at a place called St. Margaret's Hope near Edinburgh, though what name it received previous to their arrival is unknown. Noble looked the men, but sad. There were three females accompanied them and to whom the greatest courtesy was shown.— Edgar Atheling the true and rightful heir to the English throne, was the name of the principal refugee. The three ladies were his mother and two sisters Margaret and Christina. They were on their way to seek an asylum with Malcolm the Scottish King, whom they had known in England, when he was a lonely exile there. He received them all most cordially and tenderly and shortly after married the Princess Margaret, one of the two sisters of Edgar. By this union was established for all dissatisfied and exiled Saxons from England, in the reigns of William the Conqueror and of his son William Rufus, a sure haven of rest and asylum in Scotland at Malcolm's court and elsewhere, whence many of the Lowland Saxon houses derived their origin and amongst the rest the ancient *House of Borthwick.* The first of this name had come with Hengist and Horsa from their Saxon Woods and he and his successors had firmly stood by the Saxon dynasty during its continuance on the throne of England and when that house was overthrown by Normandy's great son, *Andreas Borthwick* accompanied Edgar Atheling and his two sisters to Scotland and thus planted the House of Borthwick on the waters of Borthwick not many miles from Edinburgh the "borough of Edwin" its ancient founder.

CHAPTER III.

CONTENTS.

Queen Margaret.—The Tartan—Antiquity of the Tartan by Hogg the Ettrick Shepherd.—Deaths of Malcolm and Margaret—David—Matilda—Alexander.—Malcolm II.—William the Lion.—Alexander II.—Alexander III.—The Maid of Norway.—Bruce and Baliol.—William Wallace.—His History.—Lament of Wallace, by Thomas Campbell.—The Abbot and Bruce, by Sir Walter Scott.—Romantic Adventures of Bruce.—The Brooch of Lorn, by Sir Walter Scott,—The Blood Hound.

" The Thistle waves upon the fields
   Where Wallace bore his blade,
That gave her foeman's dearest bluid
   To die her auld grey plaid.
Auld Scotland's right and Scotland's might,
   And Scotland's hills for me
I'll drink a cup to Scotland yet,
   Wi' a' the honors three.
                    REVD. H. RIDDEL."

" A third is like the former.—Filthy hags—
Why do you show me this?— A fourth—start eyes?—
What! will the line stretch out to the crack doom?—
Another yet?—A seventh?—I'll see no more—
And yet the eighth appears who bears a glass,
Which shows me many more, and some I see
That two-fold balls and treble sceptres carry,
Horrible sight!
            SHAKESPEARE'S MACBETH."

Perhaps no one was more deeply religious than beautiful Queen Margaret, the wife of Malcolm. She had been married with great pomp and splendour at Dunfermline. Gentle and lovely, with winning ways and large blue Saxon eyes she soon swayed great influence over her rough husband. The Great-Head as he was called from his name Canmore, was very apt to be sometimes fierce and passionate. Queen Margaret could always, and at all times guide him whether he were mild or fierce, and her gentle disposition did much to soften the rough exterior and grim character of King Malcolm. Though unable himself to read he would often take her beautifully Iluminated Books and fervently kiss them. He ornamented all of them with rich bindings, gold and jewels, and listened attentively when she read the sacred stories contained in them.

The Queen was fond of state and show. She always dressed in splendid apparel and at Queensferry, St. Margaret's Hope, as well as at Dunfermline kept up a royal style. She increased the number of the attendants on the Court and greatly added to the parade of the King's public appearance. She caused the royal table to be served with gold and silver plate, and encouraging the importation and use of foreign woven stuff, she was the very first who brought in the Tartan which has for the past 800 years been such a national and favorite cloth and which now seems to be again revived in the person of Lord Lorne, our new Governor General.

We must insert here the following extract from

" The Ettrick Shepherd " (Hogg) in praise of the Tartan Plaid :—

" The Plaid's antiquity comes first in view—
Precedence to antiquity is due :
Antiquity contains a certain spell,
To make e'en things of little worth excel ;
To smallest subjects gives a glaring dash,
Protecting high-born idiots from the lash ;
Much more 'tis valued, when with merit plac'd—
It graces merit, and by merit's grac'd.
  O first of garbs ! garment of happy fate !
So long employ'd, of such an antique date ;
Look back some thousand years, till records fail,
And lose therselves in some romantic tale,
We'll find our godlike fathers nobly scorn'd
To be with any other dress adorn'd ;
Before base foreign fashions interwove,
Which 'gainst their int'rest and their brav'ry
    strove.
'Twas they could boast their freedom with proud
    Rome,
And, arm'd in steel, despise the Senate's doom ;
Whilst o'er the globe their eagle they display'd,
And conquer'd nations prostrate homage paid,
They, only they, unconquer'd stood their ground,
And to the mighty empire fix'd the bound.
Our native prince, who then supplied the throne,
In Plaid array'd magnificently shone ;
Nor seem'd his purple or his ermine less,
Tho' cover'd by the Caledonian dress.
In this at court the thanes were gaily clad ;
With this the shepherds and the hynds were glad ;

In this the warrior wrapp'd his brawny arms:
With this our beauteous mothers veil'd their charms;
When ev'ry youth, and ev'ry lovely maid,
Deem'd it a dishabille to want their Plaid."

It is said that every morning Queen Margaret prepared food for nine poor orphan children, and she then fed them on her bended knees. In the evening she always washed the feet of six poor persons. She practised long fasts, which at last broke her constitution and of which she ultimately died. She had a favorite crucifix, call the Black Rood. It was of solid gold, about a hand's length. The figure of Christ was of ebony, studded and inlaid with gold. By her exertions, the Church which she established in Scotland increased and at her death she was canonized and was hereafter known as St. Margaret. Her hair,—" Her auburn hair which her bower-maidens were wont to daily dress with golden combs was long shown as a relic and having been taken abroad and kept in the College of Douay it was at last lost."

During the long reign of Malcolm, extending for thirty-six years, Scotland prospered. She held her own bravely and well during his whole reign. He came, however, to a violent end at the last. Besieging the Castle of Alnwick, with two of his sons, he was unexpectedly attacked by the English forces and he and his youngest son were slain and the army completely routed. The elder son, by name Edgar, escaped and arrived at the then residence of the King the celebrated Castle of Edinburgh. There he found his mother lying on her death bed. With a sad countenance and a dejected mien he entered the dying chamber of the good Queen. She instantly surmised the truth of his arrival.—" I know all "—she exclaimed—" tell me the truth!"

"Your husband and son are both slain" he said. The dying Queen clasped her hands in earnest prayer, but ere that prayer was ended her spirit fled and Queen Margaret was numbered with the dead.

We must now rapidly glance at the panorama of History which moves before us till the days of the father of Queen Mary, viz. James the Vth.

After the death of Malcolm, his eldest son, who had brought the news of his father's defeat at Alnwick Castle, ascended the throne and was succeeded after his death by his brother Alexander called the Fierce. Dying without children, the very youngest son of Malcolm Canmore, named David, succeeded him. His sister Matilda, called so by her sainted Mother, had for some time been married to Henry I, of England. This King was styled Beauclerk or Fine Scholar, as he was an accomplished and learned man, according to the usages of the age. In the year 1124, Alexander, another son, raised troubles but died in the Castle of Stirling. David seems to have been a politic Prince, and devoted himself to completing the pious labors of his sainted Mother and Brothers. He divided the whole country into Bishoprics, which mostly continue to this day, and founded the celebrated abbeys of Holyrood. Melrose, Dryburgh, Kelso, Jedburgh, Newbattle and Kinloss.

He was succeeded by his grand son Malcolm II, who again was followed by the celebrated William the Lion. This King died at Stirling Castle and was succeeded by Alexander II, who was followed by Alexander III. This monarch's death was somewhat remarkable. On March 12th 1286, whilst riding in the dark on a very rugged cliff near Kinghorn, his horse stumbled and he was thrown over the rocks and instantly killed. Having no children, the kingdom and throne went to the Maid of Norway. This Maid of Norway as she is styled in History was the grand daughter of Alexander II. Her mother had been married to Eric, the son of Magnus, who himself was the son of the celebrated Haco, King of Norway. Dying the year after her marriage, she left an only child who has henceforth been always styled in Scottish History "The Maid of Norway."

After this came a disputed period in the History of Scotland. Competitor after competitor arose for the Scottish crown and throne till Edward I of England decided between two claimants, Robert the Bruce and Baliol. He advanced the latter to the dignity of Scottish King requiring from him fealty and allegiance to the throne of England. The Maid of Norway had died on her way to take possession of the crown of Scotland, hence arose these troubles. The renowned Sir William Wallace united under him all patriots who detested either the English conquerors or Baliol on the Scotish throne. Wallace was no doubt one of the greatest heroes of any age, and his wonderful actions entitle him to eternal renown. Cabals arising against this disinterested patriot he was at last betrayed into the hands of the English by Menteith and shortly after beheaded and his body cruelly mangled by the enemy at London, whither he had been sent a prisoner.

The name of Wallace must ever remain among the noblest, and best of the Scottish race. The House of Elderslie had been broken up by the father, having been slain by the English soldiers and the mother taking refuge with her own people to the north of the Tay. Brooding on the ills of Scotland in general and his own house in particular, Wallace soon appeared in open rebellion against the English, the possessors of the whole country at this time. It thus happened, passing through Lanark he and his few men were sorely insulted by one of the English soldiers. This soldier having struck the sheath of Wallace's sword as a sign of challenge, the weapon of Wallace soon laid him low. He and his fellows escaped through the door of his own house in Lanark, where he at this time dwelt, and the English Governor took a vile revenge by putting his wife to death. The agony of Wallace was terrible, when he heard the news of the dreadful affliction.

"Cease, men, this is bootless pain," he said, as he saw them stand round him weeping under the greenwood boughs. They had all been extremely fond of his wife and would any one of them have died willingly to save her life. He continued and said : "We cannot bring her back to life, but no man shall ever see me rest till I have revenged the wanton slaughter of her so blithe and gay."

That very night of the murder collecting a staunch band of thirty tried warriors he silently entered Lanark. Reaching the room of the governor which communicated with the street by an outward winding stair, Wallace placed his body against the door and pressed with all his might and burst it open. The affrighted English Governor cried out: "Who makes that great deray." The deep excited voice of Wallace answered: "It is I, Wallace whom you have been seeking all day." With that he brought his sword down with such terrific force that he clave the skull of the Englishman to such an extent that the sword descended sheer to the collar bone. And although the garrison turned out, the forces of Wallace, few though they were, remained masters of the town.

This is only one of the thousand adventures of this great and patriotic man, but, at last as has been already said he was betrayed and put to a cruel and deadful death.

Here will be inserted Campbell's beautiful poem on the death of Wallace :—

They lighted a taper at dead of night,
   And chanted their holiest hymn ;
But her brow and her bosom were damp with
     affright,
   Her eye was all sleepless and dim,
And the lady of Elderslie wept for her lord,
   When a death-watch beat in her lonely room,
When her curtain had shook of its own accord,

And the raven had flapp'd at her window board,
  To tell of her warrior's doom.

Now sing ye the song and loudly pray
  For the soul of my knight so dear,
And call me a widow this wretched day,
  Since the warning of God is here,
For a night-mare rides on my strangled sleep,
  The lord of my bosom is doomed to die,
His valorous heart they have wounded deep
And the blood-red tears shall his country weep,
  For Wallace of Elderslie.

Yet knew not his country that ominous hour,
  Ere the loud matin bell was rung,
That a trumpet of death on an English tower,
  Had the dirge of her champion sung.
When his dungeon light look'd him dim and red,
  On the high born blood of a martyr slain,
No anthem was sung at his holy deathbed,
No weeping there was when his bosom bled,
  And his heart was rent in twain.

Oh! it was not thus when his oaken spear
  Was true to the knight forlorn;
And hosts of a thousand were scatter'd like deer,
  At the sound of the huntsman's horn,
When he strode o'er the wreck of each well fought field
  With the yellow-haired chiefs of his native land;
For his lance was not shiver'd, nor helmet nor shield,

And the sword that seem'd fit for archangel to
    wield,
Was light in his terrible hand.

But bleeding and bound, though the Wallace wight,
    For his much loved country die,
The bugle ne'er sung to a braver knight,
    Than Wallace of Elderslie.
But the day of his glory shall never depart,
    His head unintomb'd shall with glory be palm'd,
From his blood-streaming altar his spirit shall
    start,
Tho' the raven has fed on his mouldering heart,
    A nobler was never embalm'd.

  The spirit of liberty did not however expire with the death of Wallace. The elder Bruce died soon after the desastrous battle of Falkirk where Wallace had been defeated. but not before he had inspired his son who was a prisoner at large in the English court with the glorious resolution of vindicating his own rights and the independence of his native country.

  Bent on achieving this end, the Bruce escaped from London and with his own hand, when he had arrived at Dumfries, slew the Red Cumming, one of the most powerful and influential men in Scotland. This was a wild an unhappy deed. It caused the Bruce's position to be ten times more dangerous than before. We will now take the following extracts from one of the most popular histories of the day by the Revd. James Mackenzie:—

  " The kindly spring came on, and Bruce,

thoughtful, calm, and firm, prepared once more to try his venture. He found some friends and help among the chiefs of the Western Isles, so that he was able to assemble a little fleet of thirty-three galleys, with three hundred men on board. With these he sailed for the island of Arran. Opposite to the shore of Arran, and bounded by the blue line of the distant Scottish coast, lay his own land of Carrick. There, where he might expect support among his own vassals, he resolved to begin. His first attempt should be to recover his own castle of Turnberry from the English.

First, however, he sent over a trusty scout, a Carrick man, to look about him, to find out how the people were disposed, and what was the strength of the enemy. If he saw any fair chance of success, he was to kindle a fire upon a height above Turnberry on a certain fixed day. The day came, and Bruce walked backwards and forwards on the beach, anxiously looking towards Turnberry. The time passed, and no signal appeared. At last a faint gleam of fire showed on the sky, and quickly increased to a broad red glare. With blithesome cheer they shot their galleys into the sea, and bore away with sail and oar.

Night fell before they were midway across the channel; but they steered right for the fire, which still burned brightly over Turnberry, and soon reached the land. The scout met them on the shore. He told a gloomy tale. The English were in great force, and no good-will among the people. "Traitor," said the King, "why made you then the fire?" "Ah, sir," he said, "the fire was never made by me. I did not see it till after dark, and dreading the mistake it would lead you into, I came to meet you here and warn you of your danger." Bruce was staggered by this intelligence. Turning to his friends, he asked what they thought best to do. "I for one," said his brother Edward, "shall not return, but shall take my adventure here, whether it be good or ill." "Brother," said the king, "since you will so, we shall together take what God may send."

Percy, the English lord of Turnberry, had about two hundred of his men quartered in the village beside the castle. That night he was startled by a tumult, mingled with shouts and yells. The garrison within the castle listened to the sounds, which told of a fierce slaughter going on in the village below; but, ignorant of the enemy, they dared not venture forth in the darkness. The uproar died away, and the growing light showed the Scots dividing a rich spoil—arms, war-horses, and the whole camp equipage of the governor. Weakened as he was by the loss of so many men, the Percy was fain to keep within his gates and suffer the despite. A somewhat better beginning than the King made last year in Methven wood.

Many dark turns of fortune he had after this, however, and many a perilous adventure. The story of his adventures was written by John Barbour, a priest of Aberdeen, who lived in the reign of the Bruce and of his son. Its black-letter page, and the many words in it which are now antique and strange, render Barbour's "Life and Acts of Robert Bruce" difficult at first. But there is a noble, free spirit in it, which makes it sound stirring as the Bruce's own war-horn. Simple and primitive as it is, there was no such good English written in England itself at that time. But let us follow the king. An English force, too strong for his little band to oppose, was sent into Carrick. Bruce retired into the mountainous part of the district. The English assisted by a body of Galloway men, eagerly endeavoured to hunt him down.

One evening, when he had with him a company of only sixty, he received information that two hundred Galloway men were coming to attack him. Near by was a river, running between high and steep banks. Over this river he led his men, and posted them about two bow-shots off, on a spot of ground well secured by a morass. Here he made them rest, and returned himself with two attendants to the bank of the stream. There was but one ford, from which a steep path led up to the top of the bank, and the path was so narrow that two men could not come up together. Here the King waited and listened for some time, at length he heard the distant baying of a hound, which came every moment nearer. "I shall not disturb my weary men for the yelping of a hound," thought the King. In a little, however, he heard the noise of a body of men making straight for the ford, and instantly sent his two servants to rouse his little camp. It was a bright moonlight night, and he had a full view of his enemies as they descended the opposite bank and dashed into the ford. The first man that came up the narrow path was received with a thrust of Bruce's spear through his body. Another spear-thrust, dealt as quick as lightning, killed his horse. The fallen animal blocked up the path. Another and another of the Galloway men came on, but it was only to be rolled back on the point of that terrible spear. Those behind shouted, "On him! he cannot stand!" and more tried to rush up the steep path. Their bodies either encumbered the bank, or rolled back into the ford. By this time the assailants heard the sound of the King's men hastening to his aid. They turned and fled. The King sat down on the bank, took off his helmet, and wiped the sweat of battle from his brow. There his men found him, sitting alone in the moonlight, with fifteen corpses before him. Look at him! the moonlight, gleaming on his mail, shows a man of strong and powerful frame; the hair curls close and short round a muscular neck; the forehead is full and broad; the cheek-bones very prominent; the square and massive jaw bears the mark of some old wound; his years are about thirty. If Providence had not given us that man. Scotland at this day would have been another Ireland."

The Lord James of Douglas bethought him about this time to go over into Douglasdale, and try to snatch his own castle out of the hands of the English. Coming to the neighborhood by night, he discovered himself to a faithful vassal of his father's whom he had known in his boyhood, and who wept with joy at seeing him. In this man's house he kept close, sending secretly one by one for the trusty men who dwelt on his lands. With them he settled his plan. Palm Sunday was at hand, when the garrison of the castle would attend the neighbouring church of St. Bride. Douglas and his men took care to be there too. He had on an old cloak above his armour, and carried a flail in his hand like a countryman. His men had their weapons concealed under their mantles. The priest was busy with his ceremonies, when a voice shouted, " Douglas! Douglas!" At this signal the countryman dropped his flail and old cloak, and fell furiously with his sword on the English. His men did the same. The church rang with the clash of weapons and the din of combat. But it was soon over, and the English were all either struck down or made prisoners.

The victors proceeded immediately to the castle. The alarm had not reached it, and the gate was found open, with nobody but the porter and the cook within. Dinner for the garrison was ready, and the board was laid in the hall. Douglas ordered the gates of the castle to be shut, and sat down with his men to enjoy the feast. He then collected the arms, clothing, and valuables—all that his men could readily carry away. Next, he made them pile together in a heap all the wheat, flour, and malt found in the stores. On this heap he struck off the heads of his prisoners, and stove the casks of wine, and then set fire to the whole. All that was not stone in the castle was reduced to ashes. The country people called this terrible vengeance the " Douglas Larder."

The King, meanwhile, was pursuing his work in

the west country. He got defeats, aud gave them. His little army increased in numbers and in heart, and he felt himself able for more considerable enterprises. Early in spring he had landed in Carrick, and about the middle of May the posture of things was this : he had two English earls, whom he had defeated in the field, shut up in the castle of Ayr with the wrecks of their forces, and he was holding the castle in close siege.

Word was brought of these doings to Edward, weakened now, and shattered by age and illness. But all his fury woke afresh. He summoned his military force to meet him at Carlisle, and set out for Scotland. At Carlisle, he fancied himself so much better that he offered up the litter, in which he had travelled, in the cathedral there, and mounted on horse-back to proceed with his army. But it took him four days to ride six miles. He reached a village called Burgh-upon-Sands, from which the Scottish coast could be seen across the tossing Solway. There he had to yield to the power that conquers kings. Before he died, he called for his son, and made him swear that as soon as he was dead he would boil his body in a cauldron till the flesh separated from the bones; after which he should bury the flesh, but keep the bones; and as often as the Scots rose in rebellion, he should assemble his army and carry with him the bones of his father. So died " The Hammer of the Scottish nation," a nation which has stood a good deal of hammering. His son, happily for us, was a special fool; but he had feeling or sense enough to disregard the wish of the fierce old savage, and to send his father's body for decent burial in Westminster Abbey.

After his father's death he marched into Scotland as far west as Ayrshire, and then marched back to England again without striking a blow. Bruce, no doubt, was keenly watching to see of what metal this new Edward was made, and smiled grimly as the weakness and fickleness of the light youth appeared. Edward had retreated, but the towns and castles of Scotland were all held by English troops; and many powerful Scottish nobles, traitors to their country for the sake of their own selfish interest, were on the side of the English. King Robert had his work before him.

The northern districts, Buchan, Aberdeenshire, and Angus south to Tayside, were first cleared. As fast as the castles were taken, Bruce had them levelled with the ground. The woods and mountains were his castles, and he would not leave these great surly strengths of stone to shelter the enemy. In the south, the Lord James of Douglas freed Selkirk and Ettrick, the country of the gallant foresters who fell under Wallace at Falkirk, many of whose sons were now grown up and able to give help against the Southron. The King's brother, Edward Bruce, swept the English out of Galloway. In one year this brave captain took no fewer than thirteen castles.

It happened, on one occasion, that he received intelligence of the approach of an English force fifteen hundred strong. He made his men who were much fewer in number, take up a strong position in a narrow valley. Early in the morn-

ing, under cover of a thick mist, he set out with
fifty horsemen, and making a circuit, got unper-
ceived to the rear of the English. His intention
was to follow them cautiously under the screen of
the mist, till they should attack the troops he had
left in position, and then to fall on them from
behind. But the mist suddenly cleared away, and
discovered to the English his little party of horse
at about a bow-shot off. Edward hesitated not a
moment. With his fifty riders he charged the
English sharp and furiously, and bore many of
them down to the earth. Again, and a third time,
he charged, dashing fiercely through the English
ranks and throwing them into hopeless confusion.
They broke away in a panic and were completely
routed. It was "a right, fair point of chivalry."
Such were the men who made Scotland free.

Six years from the time that the beacon blazed
over Turnberry, Edward Bruce was engaged in the
siege of Stirling, the last fortress of any importance
remaining to the English in Scotland. The warden
of the castle, Sir Philip Mowbray, made a stout
defence. Set high on its bold rock, the castle long
defied its besiegers. At last provisions began to
fail, and the warden sent to propose a truce, bind-
ing himself to surrender the castle on mid-summer
day the next year, if not relieved before that day
by an English army. When Edward Bruce told
his brother the treaty he had made, it displeased
the King greatly. " It was unwisely done," he said
" to give such long warning to so powerful a king.
We shall be but a handful against the mighty host

that he is able to bring. God may send us fortune but we are set in great jeopardy."

"Let the King of England come," said Edward Bruce, "with all that he can call to his banner. We shall fight them all, and more!" When the King heard his brother "speak to the battle so hardily," he said, "Brother, since it is so that this thing is undertaken, let us, and all who love the freedom of this country, shape us to it manfully."

So it was resolved at all hazards to keep knightly faith, and to meet the English on the appointed day."

The murder of Comyn committed in the church of Dumfries at the Altar, was a most sacrilegious act and penance and absolution alone could atone for it. The Abbot in the following poem of Sir Walter Scott's from "The Lord of the Isles— states so:

> " Then on King Robert turned the Monk,
> But twice his courage came and sunk;
> Confronted with the hero's look,
> Twice fell his eye, his accents shook;
> At length, resolved in tone and brow,
> Sternly he questioned him,—"And thou,
> Unhappy! what hast thou to plead,
> Why I denounce not on thy deed
> That awful doom which canons tell
> Shuts Paradise, and opens Hell;
> Anathema of power so dread,
> It blends the living with the dead,
> Bids each good angel soar away,

And every ill one claim his prey;
Expels thee from the church's care,
And deafens Heaven against thy prayer.

Arms every hand against thy life,
Bans all who aid thee in the strife,
Nay, each whose succour, cold and scant,
With meanest alms relieves thy want;
Haunts thee while living, and, when dead,
Dwells on thy yet devoted head;
Rends Honour's scutcheon from thy hearse,
Stills o'er thy bier the holy verse,
And spurns thy corpse from hallowed ground,
Flung like vile carrion to the hound!
Such is the dire and desperate doom
For sacrilege, decreed by Rome;
And such the well-deserved meed
Of thine unhallowed, ruthless deed."—

" Abbot!" The Bruce replied, " thy charge
It boots not to dispute at large,
This much, howe'er, I bid thee know,
No selfish vengeance dealt the blow,
For Comyn died his country's foe,
Nor blame I friends whose ill-timed speed
Fulfilled my soon-repented deed;
Nor censure those from whose stern tongue
The dire anathema has rung.
1 only blame my own wild ire,
By Scotland's wrongs incensed to fire.
Heaven knows my purpose to atone,
Far as I may, the evil done,
And hears a penitent's appeal

From papal curse and prelate's zeal.
My first and dearest task achieved,
Fair Scotland from her thrall relieved,
Shall many a priest in cope and stole
Say requiem for Red Comyn's soul;
While I the blessed Cross advance,
And expiate this unhappy chance
In Palestine, with sword and lance.
But while content the Church should know
My conscience owns the debt I owe,
Unto De Argentine and Lorn
The name of traitor I return.
Bid them defiance stern and high,
And give them in their throats the lie!
These brief words spoke, I speak no more
Do what thou wilt; my shrift is o'er."

Like man by prodigy amazed,
Upon the King the Abbot gazed;
Then o'er his pallid features glance
Convulsions of ecstatic trance.
His breathing came more thick and fast,
And from his pale blue eyes were cast
Strange rays of wild and wandering light;
Uprise his locks of silver white,
Flushed is his brow, through every vein
In azure tide the currents strain,
And undistinguished accents broke
The awful silence ere he spoke.

" De Bruce! I rose with purpose dread,
To speak my curse upon thy head,
And give thee as an outcast o'er

To him who burns to shed thy gore;—
But, like the Midianite of old,
Who stood on Zophim, heaven-controlled,
I feel within mine aged breast
A power that will not be repressed:
It prompts my voice, it swells my veins,
It burns, it maddens, it contains!—
De Bruce, thy sacrilegious blow
Hath at God's altar slain thy foe
O'ermastered yet by high behest,
I bless thee, and thou shalt be blessed!"
He spoke, and o'er the astonished throng
Was silence, awful, deep, and long.

Again that light has fired his eye,
Again his form swells bold and high,
The broken voice of age is gone,
'Tis vigorous manhood's lofty tone:—
"Thrice vanquished on the battle-plain,
Thy followers slaughtered, fled, or ta'en,
A hunted wanderer on the wild,
On foreign shores a man exiled,
Disowned, deserted, and distressed,
I bless thee, and thou shalt be blessed!
Blessed in the hall and in the field,
Under the mantle as the shield!
Avenger of thy country's shame,
Restorer of her injured fame;
Blessed in thy sceptre and thy sword,
De Bruce, fair Scotland's rightful lord;
Blessed in thy deeds and in thy fame,
What lengthened honours wait thy name!
In distant ages, sire to son

Shall tell thy tale of freedom won,
And teach his infants, in the use
Of earliest speech, to falter Bruce.
Go, then, triumphant ! sweep along
Thy course, the theme of many a song !
The Power, whose dictates swell my breast,
Hath blessed thee, and thou shalt be blessed !"

Collecting a few patriots, among whom were his four brothers, he assumed the throne, but was defeated by the English at the battle of Methven. After this defeat he fled with some friends to the west of Scotland and the Isles where his romantic exploits and adventures would be more readable than the Arabian Knights, and where his fatigues and sufferings were as inexpressible as the courage with which he and his few friends — conspicuous among whom was the Lord Douglas, —was incredible. We have only space to give one from the prolific pen of The Wizard of the North, the other in homelier language. After passing in his retreat through Athole the Bruce arrived on the borders of the country of John, Lord of Lorne. As this John, Lord Lorne was a relation of the Red Comyn, whom Bruce had stabbed he was no frend to the Scottish King. Between Loch Awe and Loch Tay, the Highlanders met to attack him and his small company of horsemen. Moving his band slowly through the glen Bruce covered their retreat all alone. Coming to a very narrow place, suddenly, two stalwart Hilanders, brothers, and a companion, rushed upon him.

One clung to the head of his horse, another put his hands between the stirrup and boot, in order to throw the rider from the animal, the third sprung behind. The Bruce then stood upright and by his weight completely pinned the second's hands in the stirrups. He then instantly cut down the one who held his horse's head, and dashed out the brains of him who came behind and dragging the poor wretch who was held by his hands, he despatched him without opposition. It was during these perilous times that he lost the brooch or clasp of his cloak, it having been cut or torn off by one of the enemy. Sir Walter Scott alludes to the hatred of the Lord of Lorne, relative of Comyn, to Robert Bruce and the other circumstances, in the following extract taken from the well known Poem "The Lord of the Isles".

" Whence the brooch of burning gold,
That clasps the chieftain's mantle-fold,
Wrought and chased with rare device,
Studded fair with gems of price,
On the varied tartans beaming,
As, through night's pale rainbow gleaming,
Fainter now, now seen afar,
Fitful shines the northern star ?

Gem ! ne'er wrought on Highland mountain,
Did the fairy of the fountain,
Or the mermaid of the wave,
Frame thee in some coral cave ?
Did in Iceland's darksome mine,
Dwarf's swart hands thy metal twine ?

Or, mortal-moulded, comest thou here,
From England's love, or France's fear!

No!—thy splendours nothing tell
Foreign art or faëry spell.
Moulded thou for monarch's use,
By the overweening Bruce,
When the royal robe he tied
O'er a heart of wrath and pride;
Thence in triumph wert thou torn,
By the victor hand of Lorn!

When the gem was won and lost,
Widely was the war-cry toss'd!
Rung aloud Behdourish fell,
Answer'd Douchart's sounding dell,
Fled the deer from wild Tyndrum,
When the homicide, o'ercome,
Hardly 'scaped with scathe and scorn
Left the pledge with conquering Lorn!

Vain was then the Douglas brand,
Vain the Campbell's vaunted hand,
Vain Kirkpatrick's bloody dirk,
Making sure of murder's work;
Barendown fled fast away,
Fled the fiery De la Haye,
When this brooch, triumphant borne,
Beam'd upon the breast of Lorn.

Farthest fled its former Lord,
Left his men to brand and cord,
Bloody brand of Highland steel,

English gibbet, axe, and wheel.
Let him fly from coast to coast,
Dogg'd by Comyn's vengeful ghost,
While his spoils, in triumph worn,
Long shall grace victorious Lorn!"

We must insert here the story of BRUCE AND THE BLOODHOUND.

"Bruce had at one time a bloodhound, or sloth-hound, of which he was extremely fond. For a long time he made him his constant companion, caressed and fed him with his own hand; and so much did the hound love his noble master in return, that he followed his footsteps everywhere. How it came to pass we do not know, but his mortal enemy, John of Lorn, got possession of the same hound, and by this means made the Bruce run a narrower risk of losing his life than he ever did in all his other troubles and escapes. At one time he found himself hemmed in between two parties of his enemies; the English general being before him in the plain, with an army arrayed in battle; and John of Lorn coming in behind with eight hundred men, while he himself had in all only three hundred. So the Bruce, seing that he could not then fight, divided his men into three parties, and bade them each to shift for themselves as they best could. Immediately John of Lorn, who was aware of this movement, set the hound upon the scent, to find out with which party the king had gone.

"Bruce, finding himself thus pursued, divided

the hundred men who were now with him, again into three parties which again separated, and took different routes. But the poor faithful hound, little knowing that he was betraying his beloved master to destruction, still unerringly followed upon his track. "Now," said the Bruce, "it is necessary that we part from each other, and every one singly take care of himself. As for me, I will take my foster-brother with me, and we shall abide whatever fortune God may send." But this plan succeeded as badly as the former ones.

" Still did the hound, without a moment's hesitation, follow upon the track of his master; which when John of Lorn saw, he chose out five of the best men and fastest runners of his company, and bade them overtake Bruce, and by no means allow him to escape, So these five came up to the king who with his own hand slew four, while his foster-brother killed the fifth. He cared for them very little. It was the hound that he feared. He being still with the large company, might bring them all presently upon him; and though he could overcome five men, he of course could not manage five hundred. The poor king was now so overcome with weariness, through long foot-travel, and fatigue of fighting, and heaviness of spirit, that he was upon the point of giving all up, and sat him down in a wood, saying he could go no further. Then it was that a few kind words timely spoken saved a great king and a kingdom. His poor foster-brother bade him take heart, put him in mind of what was at stake, and of all that hung upon his single life, and persuaded him just to make one effort more.

"Up then the wearied warrior rose, and once more continued his way. But still the baying of the hound was borne nearer and nearer upon his ear.—if some way could not be found of putting him off that fatal scent, escape was impossible. But God's providence now interposed. Just at that spot was a stream, which came brattling through the wood clear and fast. "I have heard," said the Bruce, "that if one wade a bow-shot through a running water, it will put a hound off the track, for the scent will not lie." So his foster-brother and himself waded knee-deep with the current for a hundred yards or so, and afterwards plunged into the woods again.

"When John of Lorn came up with his large company to the place where his five men lay dead, he got into a dreadful fury, but said that presently he must have his revenge, for he knew that the king was not far off. Just then they came to the running water, and, lo! the hound for the first time began to waver—he smelt backward and forward, as if he did not know which way to go, and John of Lorn perceived that all his trouble had been in vain, and that he had best return whence he came. So it was that at this time, through God's mercy, Bruce and Scotland were saved."

CHAPTER IV.

CONTENTS:

Bruce and the Spider.—Taking of Edinburgh Castle by Sir Thomas Randolph.—Battle of Bannockburn.—The Death of De Boune.—"Bruce's Address" by Robert Burns.—Poem on "*The Battle of Bannockburn.*"

> " Let glory rear her flag of fame,
> Brave Scotland cries: "This spot I claim"—
> Here with Scotland bare her brand,
> Here with Scotland's lion stand!
> Here with Scotland's banner fly,
> Here Scotland's sons will do or die"—
> McLaggan.

" When Edward cam' down like the wild mountain flood
Wi' his chivalry prancin' in bravery;
He swore by St. George, an' his ain royal blood,
He would bring puir auld Scotland to slavery,
But our hardy blue bonnets, at fam'd Bannockburn
Ga'ed his mail-coated heroes a tussle;
An' for many lang year " Merry England " did mourn
An' bann'd baith the Scots an' their thistle.
Anon."

" Oh! land of Bruce and Wallace, of mountain and of glen
Where virtue crouns the maiden's brow, and valor moulds the men;

Long, long as thy fair heritage "the links of faith"
    shall be
Unbroken may the bonds remain that bind our
    hearts to thee.
ANON."

During these wanderings the Bruce stayed for some time in the Island of Rathlin, lying to the north of Ireland. Every one knows of the story of the spider, but there are not so many who have heard of Eliza Cook's version of the same. It is here appended, with a short account of the taking of Edinburgh Castle by Sir Walter Scott.

BRUCE AND THE SPIDER.

King Bruce of Scotland flung himself down in a
    lonely mood to think;
'Tis true he was monarch, and wore a crown, but
    his heart was beginning to sink,
For he had been trying to do a great deed to make
    his people glad,
He had tried and tried, but couldn't succeed, and
    so he became quite sad.

He flung himself down in low despair, as grieved
    as man could be;
And after a while as he pondered there, "I'll give
    it all up," said he.
Now, just at the moment, a spider dropped, with
    its silken cobweb clue,
And the king in the midst of his thinking stopped
    to see what the spider would do.

'Twas a long way up the ceiling dome, and it hung
    by a rope so fine,
That how it would get to its cobweb home, king
    Bruce could not divine.
It soon began to cling and crawl straight up with
    strong endeavour,
But down it came with a slipping sprawl, as near
    to the ground as over.

Up, up it ran, not a second it stayed, to utter the
    least complaint,
Till it fell still lower, and there it laid, a little
    dizzy and faint
Its head grew steady—again it went, and travelled
    a half yard higher,
'Twas a delicate thread it had to tread, and a road
    where its feet would tire.

Again it fell and swung below, but again it quick-
    ly mounted,
Till up and down, now fast, now slow, nine brave
    attempts were counted.
"Sure," cried the king, "that foolish thing will
    strive no more to climb,
When it toils so hard to reach and cling, and
    tumbles every time."

But up the insect went once more, ah me, 'tis an
    anxious minute,
He's only a foot from his cobweb door, oh, say will
    he lose or win it?
Steadily, steadily, inch by inch, higher and higher
    he got,

And a bold little run, at the very last pinch, put
    him into his native spot.

"Bravo, bravo!" the king cried out, "all honour
    to those who try,
The spider up there defied despair, he conquered,
    and why shouldn't I?
And Bruce of Scotland braced his mind, and gos-
    sips tell the tale,
That he tried once more as he tried before, and
    that time he did not fail.

Pay goodly heed, all you who read, and beware of
    saying "I can't,"
'Tis a cowardly word, and apt to lead to Idleness,
    Folly, and Want.
Whenever you find your heart despair of doing
    some goodly thing,
Con over this strain, try bravely again, and re-
    member the Spider and King.

"While Robert Bruce was gradually getting possession of the country, and driving out the English, Edinburgh, the principal town of Scotland, remained with its strong Castle in possession of the invaders. Sir Thomas Randolph, a nephew of Bruce, and one of his best supporters, was extremely desirous to gain this important place; but, as you well know, the Castle is situated on a very steep and lofty rock, so that it is difficult, or almost impossible, even to get up to the foot of the walls, much more to climb over them. So, while Randolph was considering what was to be done, there came to him a Scottish gentleman named Francis, who had joined Bruce's standard, and asked to speak with him in private. He then told Randolph that, in his youth, he had lived in the Castle of Edinburgh, and that his father had then been keeper of the fortress. It happened at that time that Francis was much in love with a lady who lived in a part of the town beneath the Castle, which is called the Grassmarket. Now, as he could not get out of the Castle by day to see the lady, he had practised a way of clambering by night down the Castle crag on the south side, and returning up at his pleasure; when he came to the foot of the wall he made use of a ladder to get over it, as it was not very high on that point, those who built it having trusted to the steepness of the crag. Francis had come and gone so frequently in this dangerous manner, that though it was now long ago he told Randolph he knew the road so well that he would undertake to guide a small party of men by night to the bottom of the wall, and as they might bring ladders with them, there would be no difficulty in scaling it. The great risk was that of being discovered by the watchmen while in the act of ascending the cliff, in which case every man of them must have perished.

Nevertheless, Randolph did not hesitate to attempt the adventure. He took with him only thirty men (you may be sure they were chosen for activity and courage), and came one dark night to the foot of the crag, which they began to ascend under the guidance of Francis, who went before them upon his hands and feet, up one cliff, down another, and round another, where there was scarce room to support themselves. All the while these thirty men were obliged to follow in a line, one after the other, by a path that was fitter for a cat than a man. The noise of a stone falling, or a word spoken from one to another, would have alarmed the watchmen. They were obliged, therefore, to move with the greatest precaution. When they were far up the crag, and near the foundation of the wall, they heard the guards going their rounds to see that all was safe in and about the Castle. Randolph and his party had nothing for it but to lie close and quiet, each man under the crag, as he happened to be placed, and trust that the guards would pass by without noticing them. And while they were waiting in breathless alarm, they got a new cause of fright. One of the soldiers of the Castle, wishing to startle his comrades, suddenly threw a stone from the wall and cried out, "Aha, I see you well!" The stone came thundering down over the heads of Randolph and his men, who naturally thought themselves discovered. If they had stirred, or made the slightest noise, they would have been entirely destroyed, for the soldiers above might have killed every man of them merely by rolling down stones. But, being courageous and chosen men, they remained quiet, and the English soldiers, who thought their comrade was merely playing them a trick (as, indeed, he was), passed on without further examination.

Then Randolph and his men got up, and came

in haste to the foot of the wall, which was not above twice a man's height in that place. They planted the ladders they had brought, and Francis mounted first to show them the way. Sir Andrew Grey, a brave knight, followed him, and Randolph himself was the third man who got over. Then the rest followed. As all the garrison were asleep and unarmed, excepting the watch, they were speedily destroyed. Thus was Edinburgh Castle taken in the year 1313.

Though the wife and daughters of Bruce were sent prisoners to England where the best of his friends and two of his brothers were put to death, yet he persevered till at last all Scotland save the Castle of Stirling fell into his hand. And now the 2nd Edward of England determined to subdue the rebel, as Bruce was called and succour the besieged in Stirling. With an army of—Historians declare—100,000 fighting men—the flower and the chivalry of England, he advanced towards Stirling and found Bruce encamped with the greatest judgment, near Bannockburn. The principal generals of Edward's army were the Earls of Gloucester, Hereford, Pembroke and Sir Giles Argenton. Those under Bruce were his brother, the Sir Knight of Scotland, his nephew Randolph, Earl of Murray, and the young Walter, high Steward of Scotland.

The two armies came in sight of each other on the evening of the 23rd June 1314. The Scots had about 30,000 and the English were so splendidly apparelled that their polished armour shown in the setting sun. The sharp eye of Bruce detected a large body of English cavalry cautiously advancing under cover of some gravelly knolls. Directing Randolph to oppose them, he also sent Douglas to sustain him, but Douglas perceiving that Randolph was able for the emergency, gallantly checked his own advance and left him to win the victory. As it approached evening, the Bruce mounted on a small palfrey, passed along all his line, to animate and cheer his men. The story of De Boune or De Bohun is finely told by Sir Walter Scott when describing this memorable day and heroic King in his " Lord of the Isles."

> " THE monarch rode along the van,
> The foe's approaching force to scan,
> His line to marshal and to range,
> And ranks to square, and fronts to change
> Alone he rode—from head to heel
> Sheathed in his ready arms of steel;
> Nor mounted yet on war horse wight,
> But, till more near the shock of fight,
> Reining a palfrey low and light,
> A diadem of gold was set
> Above his bright steel basinet;
> And clasped within its glittering twine
> Was seen the glove of Argentine:
> Truncheon or leading staff he lacks,
> Bearing, instead, a battle-axe.
> He ranged his soldiers for the fight
> Accoutred thus, in open sight
> Of either host.—Three bow-shots far,

Paused the deep front of England's war,
And rested on their arms a while,
To close and rank their warlike file,
And hold high council, if that night
Should view the strife, or dawning light.
Oh, gay, yet fearful to behold,
Flashing with steel and rough with gold,
  And bristled o'er with bills and spears,
With plumes and pennons waving fair,
Was that bright battle front! for there
  Rode England's king and peers:
And who, that saw that monarch ride,
His kingdom battled by his side,
Could then his direful doom foretell?—
Fair was his seat in knightly selle,
And in his sprightly eye was set
Some spark of the Plantagenet.
Though light and wandering was his glance
It flashed at sight of shield and lance.
"Knowest thou," he said, " De Argentine,
Yon knight who marshals thus their line?"—
" The tokens on his helmet tell
The Bruce, my liege: I know him well."—
" And shall the audacious traitor brave
The presence where our banners wave?—
So please my liege," said Argentine,
" Were he but horsed on steel like mine,
To give him fair and knightly chance,
I would adventure forth my lance."—
" In battle day," the king replied,
" Nice tourney rules are set aside.
" Still must the rebel dare our wrath?
" Set on him—sweep him from our path!"—

And, at king Edward's signal, soon
Dashed from the ranks Sir Henry Boune.
Of Hereford's high blood he came,
A race renowned for knightly fame.
He burned before his monarch's eye
To do some deed of chivalry.
He spurred his steed, he couched his lance,
And darted on the Bruce at once.
---As motionless as rocks that bide
The wrath of the advancing tide,
The Bruce stood fast.—Each breast beat high,
And dazzled was each gazing eye;
The heart had hardly time to think,
The eyelid scarce had time to wink,
While on the king, like flash of flame,
Spurred to full speed, the war horse came!
The partridge may the falcon mock,
If that slight palfrey stand the shock—
But swerving from the knight's career,
Just as they met, Bruce shunned the spear.
Onward the baffled warrior bore
His course—but soon his course was o'er!
High in his stirrups stood the king,
And gave his battle-axe the swing:
Right on De Boune, the whiles he passed,
Fell that stern dint—the first—the last!—
Such strength upon the blow was put,
The helmet crushed like hazel-nut;
The axe-shaft, with its brazen clasp,
Was shivered to the gauntlet grasp.
Springs from the blow the startled horse,
Drops to the plain the lifeless corse,
—First of that fatal field, how soon,
How sudden, fell the fierce De Boune!

And now the battle began. Edward attacked the Scot's army most fiercely, and it required all the courage and all the firmness of the Scottish veterans and Bruce's energy to resist it. But after a hard fought fight, the English were everywhere driven back, and one of the most complete victories recorded in history was gained. The great loss of the English fell upon the bravest part of their troops who had been led by Edward himself against Bruce in person. Some writers say the loss was 50,000 English and 4,000 Scots. The flower of the English nobility were either slain or taken prisoners. Their camp, which was immensely rich and calculated rather for a gorgeous triumph than for a hard fought campaign, fell into the hands of Bruce, and Edward himself with a few hundred noblemen, knights and cavalry fled from the battle field and never slackened pace till they came to the gates of Berwick. They escaped capture from the indomitable Douglas who eagerly pursued with only sixty horsemen, by the fleetness of their steeds arriving at Berwick. The king fled to England in a fishery boat. " *Sic transit gloria mundi.*" So long as Scottish blood circulates through Scottish veins, so long as the English language is spoken, and the name of Scotland's grandest bard—*Robert Burns*—is borne in the hearts of all true Scotchmen, on every shore and in every land, so long will his "Scot's wha hae," thrill the heart and bring the fire of martial spirit to the eye of every son of Caledonia.

BRUCE'S ADDRESS.

Scots, wha hae wi' Wallace bled,
Scots, wham Bruce has often led,
Welcome to your gory bed
    Or to victory!

Now's the day, and now's the hour,
See the front of battle lower;
See approach proud Edward's power,
    Chains and slavery!

Wha will be a traitor knave?
Wha can fill a traitor's grave?
Wha sae base as be a slave?
    Let him turn and flee!

Wha for Scotland's King and law
Freedom's sword will strongly draw,
Freeman stand or freeman fa',
    Let him follow me!

By oppression's woes and pains,
By our Sons in servile chains,
We will drain our dearest veins
    But they shall be free.

Lay the proud usurpers low!
Tyrants fall in every foe!
Liberty's in every blow!
    Let us do or die!

We finish the history of this great battle and one of the most important periods of old Scottish History with the following poem, a propos of the occasion and entitled :—

THE BATTLE OF BANNOCKBURN.

WIDE o'er Bannock's heathy wold
Scotland's deathful banners roll'd,
And spread their wings of sprinkled gold
    To the purpling east.
Freedom beamed in every eye ;
Devotion breathed in every sigh ;
Freedom heaved their souls on high,
    And steeled each hero's breast.

Charging then the coursers sprang,
Sword and helmet clashing rang,
Steel-clad warrior's mixing clang
    Echoed round the field.
Deathful see their eyeballs glare !
See the nerves of battle bare !
Arrowy tempests cloud the air,
    And glance from every shield.

Hark ! the bowman's quivering strings !
Death on grey-goose pinions springs !
Deep they dip their dappled wings
    Drunk in heroes' gore.
Lo ! Edward, springing on the rear,
Plies his Caledonian spear ;
Ruin marks his dread career,
    And sweeps them from the shore.

See how red the streamlets flow!
See the reeling, yielding foe,
How they melt at every blow!
 Yet we shall be free!
Darker yet the strife appears;
Forest dread of flaming spears!
Hark! a shout the welkin tears!
 Bruce has victory.

CHAPTER V.

CONTENTS:

Raid into England by Douglas.—Death of Robert Bruce.—Lord James Douglas.—Fight with the Moors.—The Heart of Bruce.—Origin of the House of Lockhart and of the Crests of Douglas and Borthwick.—The Legend of the Heart of Bruce, by Lady Flora Hastings.

" Scotland! Land of all I love!
Land of all that love me;
Where my youthful feet have trod,
Whose sod shall lie above me!

" England shall many a day mourn for the bloody
 [day
When blue bonnets came over the border."

SIR WALTER SCOTT.

After the decisive battle of Bannockburn, Bruce was firmly seated on his throne. His brother invaded Ireland by the request of the chieftains of Ulster and received the Irish crown in 1316. Berwick held for twenty years by the English now fell into the hands of the Scots. A raid was made into England and ended in a truce for two years. During this time the Pope was reconciled to Bruce for the murder of Comyn. The principal event of the latter years of Bruce was the celebrated Raid of Moray and Douglas into England. This happened during the reign of Edward III almost at its commencement. "They rode into England at the head of 24,000 light armed men, burdened with no camp equipage, on slight, hardy horses, each man carrying so much oatmeal and a thin plate of iron on which to bake his bannock or cake. If anything more was wanted, the country or the enemy supplied it. In vain the English with 60,000 well armed men, tried to meet them. At last they came up to the Scots posted on a ridge behind the river Wear, where it was vain in the English to attack them. They then endeavored to starve the Scots from their position, but on the morning of the fourth day, the English found the ridge empty and their enemy in a better and stronger position four miles farther away. The blockade again began, and day after day, the English persevered to break their enemy's lines by starvation. This sort of warfare was not what altogether pleased the hardy Scots as they knew that they had plenty of provisions in their camp. So one night when the English thought all secure, the Douglas with 200 picked followers crept cautiously round the English camp. At the signal the dreaded war cry of a Douglas! a Douglas! rang out in the midnight air, and Douglas and his intrepid followers reached even to the royal tent, nearly captured the king and then cut by sheer force of arm his way safely back to his own camp. Thus 18 days passed and the English thought there must be submission now, but what was their astonishment when morning broke to see the Scottish camp deserted and the enemy miles away. To show the English that they were far from starving, they left them in their camp no less than 500 slaughtered cattle which they could not drive away. 300 skin cauldrons with meat and water ready for boiling, 100 spits with beef ready to roast and 10,000 pairs of old shoes made of raw hide."

It was in this raid that the Scots first confronted fire arms and since then they have well proved how they can use them, nay, the best, the largest, the most wonderful of all modern men of war and many of the munitions of war have been made by Scotchmen in their own land, conspicuous among whom must for ever stand Robert Napier of the Glasgow Marine Foundries. The Scots called these fire arms by the curious name of "crackys of war."

At last both countries were wearied with the war. The English Parliament at York fully acknowledged the independence of Scotland, the treaty was signed at Edinburgh and Northampton, and among other things the " Black Rood" was restored (1328.)

At this period, the Holy Sepulchre and Jerusalem the "City of the World's Redemption" engrossed a very large share of attention from the piously and devoutly inclined. The Crusades had raised men's minds towards the East, and the greatest act of religion was to make a pilgrimage to the Holy Land. After many years of successful government, King

Robert Bruce, finding his end drawing near having charged the Lords of his realm to be true to his son and successor David, called to him the good Lord James of Douglas and thus spoke to him before all the assembled Peers.

"Sir James.—My dear friend, none knows better than you how great labor and suffering I have undergone in my day for the rights of this kingdom. When I was hardest beset I vowed to God that if I should live to see an end of my wars and to govern this realm in peace I would then go and make war against the enemies of Our Lord and Saviour. Never has my heart ceased to bend to this desire, but our Lord has not consented thereto, for I have had my hands full in my days, and now at the last, I am seized with this grievous sickness, so that as you all see, there is nothing for me but to die; and since my body cannot go thither, I have resolved to send my heart there in place of my body to fulfil my vow. And now dear and tried friend, since I know not in all my realm any braver knight than you, I entreat you, for the love you bear me, that you will undertake this voyage and acquit my soul of its debt to my Saviour. For I hold this opinion of your truth and nobleness that, whatever you undertake, I am persuaded you will accomplish, I will therefore, that as soon as I am dead, you take the heart out of my body and cause it to be embalmed, and take as much of my treasure as seems to you sufficient for the expenses of your journey, both for you and your companions, and that you carry my heart along with you and deposit it in the Holy Sepulchre of Our Lord, since this body cannot go thither."

At these words, all who were present wept sore. Sir James Douglas could not speak for tears. The knights, especially Borthwick and Lockhart were much distressed. At last Sir James replied—"Ah, most gentle and noble king, a thousand times I thank you for the great honour you have done me, in making me the bearer of so precious a treasure. Most faithfully and willingly, to the best of my power, shall I obey your commands."

"Ah, gentle knight," said the king—" I heartily thank you, provided you promise to do my bidding, on the word of a true and loyal knight."

"I do promise my liege" replied Douglas by the "faith which I owe to God and to the order of "knighthood."

"Now God be praised" said the king "for I shall die in peace, since I know, that the best and most valiant knight of my kingdom will perform that for me which I myself could never accomplish."

Shortly after this, the violence of his disease still increasing, death fast approached and the noble king departed his life in the fifty-fifth year of his age. A fair tomb of pure white marble was erected in the choir of the Abbey of Dunfermline, where they laid their most illustrious dead. Never was funeral more numerously attended, nor weeping crowds more heart-stricken—"Alas" they cried, "he is gone whose wisdom and might compelled our enemies to respect us, and made our name honourable in all lands," Bishop and prelate, knight and squire, noble and vassal were all there. The funeral chant by the monks of the Abbey rose and swelled beneath the massive arches and vaults of the ever sombre aisles. But ever and anon, amidst the pauses of the funeral dirge, the voice of lamentation and weeping from the stately as well as from the common throng, arose and was wafted far upon the breeze. Well might they weep, prophetically, for the day was near at hand when they would miss him right sore and never did Scotland again see one so deeply mourned.

Obedient to the dying request of his king, the Lord James Douglas, departed for the Holy Land being accompanied by a fair and goodly band of knights, esquires and followers. He bore the heart of Bruce enshrined in a silver casket about his neck.

On his passage to the East he learned that Alphonso, king of Spain, was waging war against the Saracens, those Moors, who were such determined foes to the Holy Sepulchre and Jerusalem. Supposing he was called to help the Christian against the Moslem, Sir James joined the Spaniards, when the two armies met shortly after close by Gibraltar. Alphonso gave to Lord Douglas the command of the centre division. The Scots bravely headed the charge which was made with such success that the enemy was routed and their camp taken. While the Spaniards were engaged in plunder, the Scottish leader, at the head of the small band of his own knights and warriors, pursued the flying Infidels. But before he was aware, the Saracens rallied, and he was surrounded by a dense crowd of cavalry which every moment grew thicker and thicker. When Douglas saw Sir William St. Clair of Roslyn with his brave knights and especially Lockhart and Borthwick fighting desperately, " Yonder worthy knight will be slain," he said "unless he have instant help" and galloped to his rescue. Taking from his neck, the silver casket, containing the heart of Bruce, he threw it with all his strength into the very thickest of the enemy, crying out "Now pass thou onward as thou wert wont, and Douglas will follow thee or die." With this he made a furious charge and soon cleared a space about him. But vain was his valor, overwhelmed by numbers, he fell, the good Sir James, covered with many wounds.

After the fray, the silver casket was found near to the spot where he fell. His surviving knights took him up with reverent care. His flesh was separated from his bones and buried in holy ground in Spain. His bones were brought home to Scotland and buried in his own church of Douglas.

Many of the followers of Douglas were slain in the battle in which he fell. The rest resolved not to proceed to Palestine but to return to Scotland. One of the knights was entrusted to carry back the heart of Bruce, whence the House of Lockhart derive their name. Since this period, the Douglases have always carried upon their shield a bloody heart with a crown upon it, and Borthwick, one of the bravest of the Douglas' knights received permission to place a Moor's Head on his escutcheon as a memento of his fight in Spain, which emblem is still the crest of the House of Borthwick and took the motto " Qui Conducit" as a memorial of that day. and the descendants of the original Borthwick who had come a blue eyed Saxon with Hengist and Horsa to England's shores, and who with Edgar and

Margaret sought protection with the Scottish King Canmore, now rested for a little from their toils and gradually grew opulent and well known after the death of Bruce.

We append the following beautiful poem on the legend of the Heart of Bruce, by Lady Flora Hastings.

> A GALLEY seeks the port of Sluys,
>   And o'er the azure wave
> Rode never bark more fair than she,
>   More royal, and more brave.
> The white sails swelling to the breeze
> Are mirrored in those summer seas,
> As ocean birds with snowy wing
> O'er the blue deep their shadows fling;
> And round the prow the dancing spray
> Blushes to catch the sunny ray,
> And melts in ambient air away.
>
> High on the prow a warrior band
> In trim array are seen to stand;
> Banner and pennon, sword and spear,
> And mace and battle-axe are there;
> And crested helm, and armour bright,
> Buckler and baldric richly dight.
> They do not come with sword and lance,
> To devastate the fields of France,—
> Nor, led by policy, resort
> A mission to King Philip's court:
> They come not with rich merchandise
>   To seek the crowded mart;
> But pilgrims to Jerusalem,
>   They bore King Robert's heart.

And chief among the gallant throng
Was Douglas—he for whom so long
Woke the wild harp of Scottish song;
Whom still a fond tradition names
With benison, "The good Sir James."—
He was both bold and blithe of mood,
Of faith unstained, and lineage good;
Loyal of heart and free of hand
As any knight in Christian land;
Fair largess he to minstrels gave,
And loved the faithful and the brave.
So many graces did commend
The knight who was King Robert's friend.

 * * * * * *

For as in gray Dunfermline's tower
 He stood beside the bed
Whereon, in life's departing hour,
 Was good King Robert laid,
Whose failing breath and nerveless form
Bespoke him brother of the worm,
While visions of the days gone by
Flitted before his glazing eye,
And the old monarch's failing breath
Spoke of the fast approach of death—
Brave Douglas kissed the feeble hand
That once had fought for fair Scotland,
 And pledged his knightly word
That he the Bruce's heart would bear
Unto the Holy Sepulchre
 Of our most Blessed Lord.

KING ALPHONSO AND DOUGLAS.

"I pray you by your knighthood's oath,
    And by the cross you wear,
And by your master's dying 'hest,
    And by your lady fair;
I pray you by your courtesy,
    To lend our cause your blade;—
Flower of the Scottish chivalry,
    Come to the Cross's aid!"

Out spake the gentle Douglas then :— " I may not, by my vow,
Thus summoned to the Cross's aid, the holy strife forego.
But, oh! thou distant Solyma, long space it must be ere,
A pilgrim, I shall bend my knee beside the Sepulchre.
Oh, that I first might seek the land of our Blessed Saviour's birth,
And lay my honoured master's heart in Syria's holy earth!
And lave, by Jordan's sainted stream, my care-worn, furrowed brow,
Ere sword again I draw.—Enough! I may not, for my vow!"

   *   *   *   *   *   *

On rushed the Douglas—never knight
More valiant sought the field of fight.
Amidst the fray his snowy crest
Danced like the foam on ocean's breast;

Like lightning brand his broad-sword flashed,
And foemen bent and targets crashed!
With stalwart arm and giant form
He charged like spirit of the storm!
And—as upon the mountain side,
So late the trackless forest's pride,
Uprooted by the wintry blast,
The prostrate sapling oaks are cast—
Lo! where he spread his dread career,
Bent Moslem crest and Moslem spear;
While ever, 'midst the mêlée, high
And clear pealed forth his battle cry.
It seemed, indeed, a spell of power
Nerved Douglas' arm that fatal hour;
For, lo! to his faithful bosom pressed,
  In its jewelled casket of orient gold,
The heart that once throbbed in the Bruce's breast
  Was borne into fight by that baron bold.
Marvel ye, then, that his arm was strong?
That he humbled the pride of the Moslem throng?
That where'er he turned, from his dreaded track
The Moors, in their wild dismay, drew back?

    *   *   *   *   *   *

"Pass on, brave heart, as thou wert wont
  Th' embattled hosts before:
Douglas will die, or follow thee
  To conquest, as of yore!"
They met—they closed; dread was the strife,—
More dear the gage than fame or life:
There, foot to foot, and hand to hand,
They stood opposed, and brand crossed brand!
Steel rang on steel—the war-steeds' tread

Trampled the dying and the dead;
The lurid clouds of dust on high
Rose eddying to the darkened sky;
The vulture snuffed the scent of blood,
And, screaming, roused her loathsome brood.
But the pale Crescent waned—the host
Of Osmyn saw the battle lost;
And loath to fly, but forced to yield,
Abandoned sullenly the field.

Where was the Douglas?—On the plain
They found him, 'midst the heap of slain.
Faithful in death, his good right hand
Held with firm grasp his broken brand;
While, o'er the sacred casket laid,
A bulwark of his corse he made.
And deem ye not, though fallen there,
The dying Douglas breathed a prayer
For that far land he loved the best,—
The land where Bruce's ashes rest;—
For Scotland's worth, and Scotland's weal;
For truth to guide, for peace to heal;
For freedom and for equal laws,
And men to strive for freedom's cause?

The fane is fallen—the rite is o'er—
The choral anthem peals no more;
The moonbeam strays through nave and aisle,
And the verdant ivy clings round the pile.
It recks not—like dew 'neath the sunny ray,
The crumbling fabric may pass away;
It recks not—for deep in the patriot's breast
The names of his country's heroes rest;
And a thrill of pride it will aye impart,
That Scottish earth wraps the prince's heart.

THE TWO LIONS.

King Robert Bruce was very fond of animals and the story of his blood-hound is already recorded but it is not so well known that he was remarkably partial to a large royal Lion, which quite tame, followed him like a dog. The following poem composed by the Author of these Sketches, speaks of them both in the title of THE TWO LIONS.

I look far down the stream of time and what do I behold
Athwart my vision, facing me, I see two lions bold,
The one auld Scotias' hero, who bravely fought and bled,
The other his companion, from Afric forest led,
The hero's eye is dim and dull,—but yet it is not age,
The other's eyes are glittering, but no leonine rage
Is seen therein, for tamely he follows his good lord,
Or licks his hand or gambols at his loved masters' word;
The mighty Bruce has vanquished all his loved country's foes,
And in the past are buried all Scotia's wrongs and woes,
And now afflicted with disease, at Cardross Castle he
Calmly awaits the Conqueror of all Humanity.
He has achieved the liberty, independence and the crown
Of his loved land, and now awaits the time to lay them down.

Yet I look still further back, and see the mighty
  Bruce alone
Fleeing like a very fugitive, all his friends and followers gone;
But the God of Battles kept him in his darkest
  blackest hour,
That the blessing of the patriot on his children
  he might pour;
That the mighty Scottish warrior by his countrymen should be
Remembered in all ages, and through all posterity.
Ah! my soul is stirred within me as I behold this
  sight,
And memory brings before me, the field of Bannocks' fight,
I see the noble Bruce and his army sworn to die,
Or else achieve, from England, a glorious victory,
I see the emblazoned banner of the Scottish Lion
  bold,
Unfurl to the western breeze, its glittering golden
  fold;
And I hear the shout of battle and I see the Bannock plain
Covered and crowded thickly, with the English
  army slain,
And I hear a mighty noise at each bend and every
  turn,
Of the Scottish victors shouting, "The Bruce of
  Bannockburn."
Yet the grandest sight of all is, when these great
  Lions two
Walk together or recline beneath the spreading
  Cardross yew;

The one, auld Scotia's monarch, of whom ages yet
    will sing,
The other Scotia's emblem, and of forest beasts,
    the king.

CHAPTER VI.

CONTENTS:

The Feudal System—Lord and Vassal.

During the reign of Malcolm the Great Head, the Feudal System began in Scotland. It took a very long time to become general, and never attained universal sway. The mode of renting lands at this time differed considerably from that of the present day. Tenants held their lands on condition of being ready to fight for their Lord whenever they were required and to bring into the field a certain number of retainers, according to their rental.

The crown vassals or nobles who held lands from the king, granted estates to knights and esquires and gentlemen upon the same terms of military service; as for instance, the Barons of Borthwick and of Pennicuik were vassals or knights in the retinue of St. Clair, the Earl of Roslyn, the one being his cup bearer, the other his carver. These sub-vassals again, gave land to an inferior class of proprietors, yeomen, who were also bound to follow their Lord into the field. Thus the king was at liberty to call out his vassals, the nobles: then the nobles could call out their vassals, the gentlemen;

the gentlemen could call out their vassals, the yeomen. When the king gave his order, the whole machinery of the feudal system was instantly set in motion.

These vassals, were obliged to provide their own fighting accoutrements. The gentlemen rode on heavy war chargers. Completely encased in steel armor, they looked like iron men on horseback. When the visor was shut, the face was altogether hidden and nothing was discernable save a pair of fierce eyes gleaming through the apertures. The shield, generally of polished steel and sometimes inlaid with gold and silver, hung by a belt round the neck. Their weapons consisted of lance, heavy sword, battle-axe, and club or mace of steel. The yeomen fought on foot. They wore a morion or iron-cap and a jack or leathern jacket well quilted with splints of iron. Axe, spear and dagger completed their armour.

A great percentage of the population on the feudal estates were slaves or serfs. These serfs were bound to stay on their master's land and if they ran away or left it they were brought back like oxen or sheep which have strayed, and punished accordingly. Their work consisted in felling timber, carrying manure, repairing roads and such like. Anything which they might possess might be taken by their Lord. He could sell them like cattle, as they were his own property as much as the beasts of his stall. The power of the feudal Lord over these poor wretches was great. As it was called in those days, he had the power of pit and gallows over them, that is, he could drown the women and hang the men, on account of which a tree used for the latter purpose and called the Dule-tree or Tree of Sorrow, usually stood near by the castle walls.

When the grant of an estate was made the vassal performed homage to the Lord as an expression of his obedience and submission. The head was uncovered, the belt ungirt, the sword and spurs removed, then kneeling, he placed his hands between those of the Lord and promised to be his man from henceforth to serve him with life and limb and all worldly honor, faithfully and to the end. Then the ceremony concluded with a kiss.

As soon as possible if there were not a castle already built, the feudal lord commenced to build his castle. He always looked out for some secure spot, on the top of a crag, or hill. or even sometimes in the midst of a bog or marsh. The building generally consisted of a grim, massy tower or keep with outbuildings and the whole surrounded by a strong fortified wall and a ditch or moat only passable by means of a narrow draw-bridge. This moat occasionally was filled with water, sometimes it was empty, but either way formed a sure defence. In this rude habitation the Lord dwelt with his family and retainers in wild magnificence. Every day in the great stone hall, the household board was spread out in profuseness and splendor, the Lord sitting at the head of the long oaken table, while the fumes of meat boiled, roasted and stewed, hid the roof of the sombre hall, and tall, black bearded and armed men passed round and round the goblets and pitchers of home-made ale. Under the table and around, the dogs, always in considerable numbers, growled and fought over the offal and bones among the rushes and the straw with which the room was strewn. Not far from the tower and easily heard by the warden's horn the serfs dwelt together in a clachan or village of huts.

The feudal Lord was judge of each and every cause within his own bounds, and feudal justice was none of the strictest. The decision of the Lord was imperative and must be obeyed.

It was a gay and pleasing sight when the Baron and his retainers rode out to hunt. Then the priest said the hunting mass in the Chapel, and amidst the baying of the deer-hounds and the champing bits of the steeds, the Baron arrived in the court yard. The ladies next came and they were helped with kind courtesy upon their palfreys. Then the whole cavalcade swept away over the plain or into the forest, to hunt the deer or fly their hawks.

Gay too was the sight, when the pomp of war issued forth from the Castle gates. In front rode the liege lord with his banner borne before him and followed by his knights, each one attended by his own pennon and men-at-arms. The burnished steel of their armour gleamed brightly in the sun, and amidst the din of trumpets, the snuffing of the coursers and the waving of scarfs from battlement and bartizan, held by the hands of the fair inmates left behind, the troop rode on to victory or death.

Such was the feudal system, which lasted so long in England and Scotland, and such with more or less difference, is the history of each individual house of ancient Caledonia; a system which repeatedly plunged both countries in civil war, and at last wrought its own ruin, a system which even appeared a little more than a hundred years ago, when Prince Charles Stuart attempted to regain the throne of his ancestors, but failed, after the bloody battle of Culloden.

CHAPTER VII.

CONTENTS:

David II.—Battle of Halidon.—The Knight of Liddesdale. —Robert II.— Otterburn or Chevy Chase.— John or Robert III.—Title of Duke first used.—Another raid into England.—Henry Hotspur.—Extracts from Shakespeare's 1st Part of Henry IVth.

Douglas.—" Another king! they grow like hydras heads."
SHAKESPEARE.

Immediately after the death of Bruce family feuds and quarrels arose regarding the crown. At last however David II, son of the king, by his second wife ascended the throne, being crowned at Scone, by the Bishop of St. Andrews. During his reign was fought the Battle of Halidon Hill where the Scots suffered a crushing defeat from the English and with the defeat the loss of Berwick.

It was also in this king's reign that the Douglas called the Knight of Liddesdale and Flower of Chivalry was slain by his kinsman Lord William whilst he was hunting in Ettrik. David being a weak prince, was taken prisoner by the English at the battle of Neville's Cross, and was ransomed and died in Edinburgh Castle, 1371.

Robert II was 55 years old when he succeeded to the Scottish throne. He was the first of the Line of Stuart. During his reign was fought the celebrated battle of Otterburn or Chevy Chase. The occasion of this event was this. The Scots resolved to invade England on account of a raid which the Earls of Northumberland and Nottingham had made in 1383. The Douglas with 300 picked lances and 2000 infantry was sent against the east part of England. He advanced to the gates of Durham and returned laden with booty. The Earl of Northumberland sent his son Sir Henry named by the Scots Hotspur against him. By some mishap the pennon of Hotspur was secured by Douglas who boasted he would place it on his tower at Dalkeith. Hotspur declared it should never go out of Northumberland. Douglas placed it before his tent and bade him come and take it.

The friends of Hotspur kept him back that night from attempting to regain his pennon. In the meantime the Scots were on their way home whilst Douglas fancied when the army arrived at Otterburn, that his honour was not complete if he did not give Hotspur a chance of regaining his pennon. So entrenching a camp the wearied Scots taking off their armour lay down to rest. But during the night Hotspur attacked the camp with 800 men at arms and 8000 foot. Then the Scots, roused from their sleep, soon attacked the foe and Douglas seizing an axe in both hands cleared a space around him till he was borne down and trodden on, neither friend nor foe knowing he had fallen. Dying he ordered his troops still to shout the Douglas cry, and the result was that the English were driven back, Harry Hotspur being made a prisoner. The loss of the English was great, that of the Scots but small. Shortly after this the King died in the Castle of Dundonald, near Irvine, an old man and a peaceable king.

He was succeeded by his son John, but this name was detested by the Scots so it was changed to the popular one of Robert. It was during the reign of Robert III that a new title was introduced into Scotland. The King's brother was made the *Duke* of Albany and his eldest son was called *Duke* of Rothesay. This is the first instance of the title being used.

Another raid into England occurred during Roberts' reign which must be noted. It was also headed by the Douglas. He advanced with 10,000 men into Durham and was returning laden with plunder when Henry Hotspur met him at Homildon Hill. Percy played upon the solid mass of Scottish spearmen with his arrows and to such an extent that the Scots were totally defeated and Douglas taken prisoner. As Percy had been before released when taken by a raid so Douglas was also released.

Shortly after he joined the forces of the Earl of Northumberland and Hotspur who had rebelled against their king, Henry IVth, but he was again made prisoner at the celebrated Battle of Shrewsbury.

Let us cull a little from Shakespear's beautiful play of the 1st part of Henry IVth relating to Douglas and Hotspur and allow the immortal Bard of Avon to carry on the history of these two celebrated warriors. Scene III of the 5th Act introduces us to the Plains of Shrewsbury where Douglas and Sir Walter Blunt a friend of the English king meet.

Blunt.—What is thy name, that in the battle thus
    Thou crossest me? what honor dost thou seek
  Upon my head?
Douglas.—Know then, my name is Douglas
  And I do haunt thee in the battle thus,
  Because some tell me that thou art a king.
Blunt.—They tell thee true,
Douglas.—The Lord of Stafford dear to-day hath bought,
  Thy likeness, for, instead of thee, King Harry
  This sword hath ended him, so shall it thee
  Unless thou yield thee as my prisoner.
Blunt.—I was not born a yielder, thou proud Scot
  And thou shall find a King, that will avenge
  Lord Stafford's death.

They fight and Blunt is slain, enter Hotspur.

Hotspur.—Oh! Douglas, hadst thou fought at Holmedon thus,
  I never had triumph'd upon a Scot.
Douglas.—All's done, all's won, here breathless lies the king.

Hotspur.—Where?
Douglas.—Here.
Hotspur.—This, Douglas? I know this face full well,
A gallant knight he was, his name was Blunt
Semblably furnish'd like the king himself.
Douglas.—A fool go with thy soul, whither it goes,
A borrowed title hast thou bought too dear,
Why didst thou tell me that thou wast the king?
Hotspur.—The king hath many marching in his coats.
Douglas.—Now, by my sword, I will kill all his coats,
I'll murder all his wardrobe piece by piece
Until I meet the king.
Hotspur.—Up and away;
Our soldiers stand full fairly for the day.

Enter the king, alarums, enter Douglas.

Douglas.—Another king, they grow like Hydra's heads;
I am the Douglas, fatal to all those,
That wear those colors on them, what art thou
That counterfeit'st the person of a king?
King Henry.—The king himself, who, Douglas grieves at heart,
So many of his shadows thou hast met
And not the very king, I have two boys
Seek Percy and thyself about the field,
But seeing those fall'st on me so luckily
I will assay thee, so defend thyself.

Douglas.—I fear thou art another counterfeit
 And yet, in faith, thou bear'st thee like a king,
 But mine, I am sure, thou art, whoe'er thou be
 And thus I win thee. *They fight.*

Enter Prince Henry, the King being in danger.

Prince Henry.—Hold up thy head, vile Scot, or thou art like,
 Never to hold it up again, the spirits
 Of Shirly, Stafford, Blunt, are in my arms
 It is the Prince of Wales, that threatens thee;
 Who never promiseth, but he means to pay.

They fight, Douglas flies.

 Cheerly, my lord; how fares your grace?
King Henry.—Stay and breathe awhile
 I'll go to Sir Nicholas Gawsey.

Exit King Henry, enter Hotspur.

Hotspur.—If I mistake not, thou art Harry Monmouth.
Prince Henry.—Thou speak'st as if I would deny my name.
Hotspur.—My name is Harry Percy.
Prince Henry.—Why, then I see
 A very valiant rebel of the name.
 I am the Prince of Wales; and think not, Percy,
 To share with me in glory any more,

Two stars keep not their motion in one sphere,
Nor can one England brook a double reign
Of Harry Percy and the Prince of Wales.
Hotspur.—Nor shall it Harry, for the hour is come
To end the one of us, and would to God,
Thy name in arms were now as great as mine.
Prince Henry.—I'll make it greater, ere I part from thee
And all the budding honors on thy crest,
I'll crop, to make a garland for my head.
Hotspur.—I can no longer brook thy vanities.

They fight and Hotspur is wounded and falls.

Oh! Harry, thou has robb'd me of my youth,
I better brook the loss of brittle life,
Than those proud titles thou hast won of me,
They wound my thoughts, worse than thy sword my flesh,
But thought's the slave of life; and life, time's fool,
And time, that takes survey of all the world,
Must have a stop, oh, I could prophesy
But, that the earthy and cold hand of death
Lies on my tongue—No—Percy—thou art dust
And food for—— *dies.*
Prince Henry.—For worms, brave Percy. Fare thee well, great heart;

Ill-weaved ambition how much art thou
                                    shrunk!
When that this body did contain a spirit
A kingdom for it was too small a bound,
But now, two paces of the vilest earth
Is room enough, this earth, that bears thee
                                    dead,
Bears not alive so stout a gentleman,
If thou wert sensible of courtesy,
I shonld not make so dear a show of zeal;
But let my favors hide thy mangled face,
And even in thy behalf, I'll thank myself
For doing these fair rites of tenderness;
Adieu, and take thy praise with thee to
                                    Heaven,
Thy ignominy sleep with thee in the grave,
But not remembered in thy epitaph.

Another part of the field.—*Enter King Henry, Prince Henry, Prince John, Westmoreland and others.*

King Hénry.— Thus ever did rebellion find rebuke,
    How goes the field?
Prince Henry.—The noble Scot, Lord Douglas when
                                    he saw
The fortune of the day quite turned from
                                    him,
The noble Percy slain and all his men
Upon the foot of fear, fled with the rest,
And falling from a hill, he was so bruis'd
That the pursuers took him. At my tent
The Douglas is and I beseech your grace
I may dispose of him.

King Henry.—With all my heart.
Prince Henry.—Then, brother John of Lancaster
to you,
This honorable bounty shall belong,
Go to the Douglas and deliver him,
Up to his pleasure, ransomless and free,
His valor, shown upon our crests to-day,
Hath taught us how to cherish such high
deeds,
Even in the bosom of our adversaries.

CHAPTER VIII.

CONTENTS:

James I.—Death of his father.—James taken to England.
—Sir William de Borthwick.—Borthwick Castle. and
Borthwick Church.—The Earl of Lennox.—Sir Robert
Graham.—Death of the King at Perth.—Brave Lady
Douglas. — Punishment of the Conspirators, from
"Drummond's Scotland" 1681.

THE young Prince James of Scotland being now about 14 years of age, it was thought advisable to send him to France for education and training. He sailed with a gallant retinue from the Forth, but shortly after was captured by an English war vessel. This preyed upon the susceptibilities and nerves of the King to such a degree that he died next year 1406, at Rothesay, leaving the kingdom to his son James.

When James arrived in England he was first sent to the Tower of London and afterwards went to France in the train of Henry Vth.

He remained for many years a state prisoner in England, at last a movement was made to bring him back, one of the principal gentlemen connected with it being William the 1st Lord Borthwick.

SIR WILLIAM DE BORTHWICK was a Commissioner A. D. 1411 and 1413 for treating with the English and *William Dominus de Borthwick*, A. D. 1421, was one of the hostages for the return of James I when it was proposed that his Majesty should visit Scotland on parole. A safe conduct too was granted to *William de Borthwick de eodem miles*, to proceed to England as a commissioner to treat for the release of James the First, May 1423, and next year another safe conduct to *William de Borthwick, Dominus de Herriot* to repair to England to meet his Majesty when released. When the King returned, at the baptism of his twin sons, James I created several knights and among the rest *William the 1st Lord Borthwick* son of that *Sir William Borthwick* who had helped him in his exile. This first Lord Borthwick then was sent to England as one of the hostages for the payment of the balance of the ransom money ;£10,000 being taken off it when the King had married the beautiful daughter of the Earl of Somerset. *Lord Borthwick* remained exactly two years in England and the ransom being paid he returned, and received from the King a charter under the great seal and license to build a castle which he did and called it BORTHWICK CASTLE.

This Castle became the chief residence of the family and gave its name to the surrounding country or parish. " Like many other baronial residences in Scotland he built this magnificent pile upon the very verge of his property." William de Hay, from whom *Sir William Borthwick* had acquired a part of his estate, looked with envy upon the splendid castle of his neighbor and vented his spleen by building a mill upon his own lands close to the Castle and indeed immediately beneath the knoll on which the fortress was situated, declaring that the Lord of Borthwick in all his pride should never be out of the hearing of the clack of his neighbour's mill. The mill still exists, whilst the lordly castle is slowly falling into ruins. The Castle consisted principally of a vast square tower, with square and round bastions at equal distances from its base. The walls are thirteen feet thick near the bottom and towards the top gradually contracted to six feet. Besides the sunk story the walls are 90 feet high from the adjacent area to the battlement and if the roof were included, the whole height was 110 feet. Nisbet says : " The great hall is 40 feet long and so high in the roof that a man on horseback might turn a spear in it with all the ease imaginable."

At this period the Church of Kentigern now Borthwick was built. This church of Borthwick is one of the oldest architectural buildings (now in ruins) in Scotland. It consisted of a nave and chancel with a semicircular termination. Although quite roofless and much ruinated the apse is comparatively entire. The arch is of two orders. There are three plain and large round-headed lights with wide internal splays, disposed in the usual manner, the east one is blocked, that on the north is covered in the interior by a very elegant ornamental arched recess and canopy containing a high tomb, bearing the recumbent effigies of a knight in armour the Lord Borthwick and his lady clothed in a long flowing robe on his left, their hands clasped and faces turned to the east.

A small mortuary chapel probably erected at the same period as the monument, is appended to the north of the chancel. This is entire and covered in with a pointed roof paved externally with large overlapping stone flags arranged diamond-wise. A pretty large transeptal chapel of two bays is also nearly perfect. Borthwick Church contains what very few of the old churches do, a very fair preserved apse, which is a very characteristic and now extremely rare feature of the oldest class of churches existing in Scotland. This church has therefore the Benaturæ, Piscinæ, Easter Sepulchre and Monument.

The King after his return to Scotland, executed the old Earl of Lennox on the "Heading hill," at Stirling (1425). Having given this striking example of vigour, James set himself to remove the misrule of his country and to "make the key keep the castle and the bracken bush the cow."

It is impossible for any ruler to make reforms and not incur hatred from some of his subjects, so with James. Sir Robert Graham offended the King and even called him a tyrant in Parliament. For this he fled to the Highlands and the King set out to chastise these turbulent Caledonians and thus he put himself into their power. On Christmas, 1436 he held his court in the Blackfriars at Perth, and continued merry making and hunting till the 20th July 1437. On this night 300 Highlanders crossed the moat and tried to break into the monastery. The Ladies sprung up to fasten the door but the bolts had been removed and one of them, heroic woman that she was thrust her plump white arm through the staples of the door. Brave Lady Douglas had her arm crushed and broken by the conspirators who entered soon after. They found the poor King hid in a kind of hole or cellar, in the floor and Graham and others descending slew James with 28 deadly wounds. Thus fell the first of the name of James. But the King was adored by the people and bitter and terrible was their vengeance. Almost all the conspirators suffered violent deaths and the " Milk-white dove," became the destroying eagle and crushed remorselessly those who had murdered her Lord and Master. Quoting from an old Scottish History on the table before me, and called " Drummond's Scotland," published A.D. 1681 in London, he says of the murder of this King : " The rumour of this Murther blazed abroad, it is incredible what weeping and sorrow was through all the country, for even by them to whom his Government was not pleasant, he was deplored and the act thought execrable. The Nobles of their own accord and motion from all parts of the kingdom assembled and came to Edinburgh and ere they consulted together (as if they had all one mind) directed troops of armed men through all the quarters of the kingdom, to apprehend the Murtherers and produce them to justice. Such diligence was used (grief and anger working in their minds) that within the space of forty days all the conspirators were taken and put to shameful deaths. The common sort, as *Christopher Clawn or Cahoun* and others that were of the Council of the Conspiracy, having had art or part in the plot were hanged on gibbets. The chief actors, that the Commonwealth might publicly receive satisfaction, were made spectacles of justice by exquisite torments. The punishment of *Athol* was continued three days. On the first he was stript naked to his shirt, and by a crane fixed to a cart, often hoisted aloft, disjointed, and hanging shown to the people, and thus dragged along the great street of the town; on the second day he was mounted on a pillar in the Marquet place, he was crowned with a diadem of burning iron, with a plachart bearing: *The King of all Traytors;* thus was his oracle accomplished; on the third day he was laid naked along upon a scaffold, his belly was ript up, his heart and bowels taken out and thrown in a fire flickering before his eyes. Lastly his head was cut off and fixed in the most eminent place of the town, his body sent in quarters to the most populous cities of the kingdom to remain a trophy of justice.

His nephew *Robert Stuart* was not altogether so rigorously handled, for that he did but consent to others wickedness, being only hang'd and quarter'd.

But for that it was notorious, *Robert Graham* had embrewed his hands in the King's blood, a gallows being raised in a cart, he had his right hand nailed to it, and as he was dragged along the street, executioners, with burning pincers, tearing the most fleshly parts of his carcass, being nip'd, torn, and stay'd, his heart and entrails were thrown in a fire, his head exalted and his quarters sent amongst the Towns, to satisfy the wrath and sorrow of the injured people; being asked during his torture how he dared put hand in his Prince, he made answer that having Heaven and Hell at his choice, he dared leap out of Heaven and all the contentments thereof, in the flaming bottoms of Hell,—an answer worthy such a traitor.

Œneas Sylvius then Legate in Scotland for Pope Eugenius the fourth (after Pope himself) having seen this sudden and terrible revenge, being a witness of the execution, said he could not tell whether he should give them " greater commendations that revenged the King's death, or brand them, with sharper condemnation that distain'd themselves with so hainous a parricide."

CHAPTER IX.

CONTENTS.

James II.—His birth.—The Lord of Lorne.—Wars of the Roses.—Death of the "Milk White Dove."—Siege of Roxburgh.—Death of James.

HIS son James II was only six years old when his father was sssassinated. He was crowned at Holyrood Abbey in Edinburgh, as Scone, the real place for such ceremonies was too near the scene of his father's murder. The "Milk White Dove" stayed at Stirling Castle, and her young son in Edinburgh Castle, but afterwards for more security she visited him and had him conveyed in a box to the Castle of Stirling then commanded by Sir Alexander Livingston. At this time the Earl of Douglas died, and the Douglas estates fell into the hands of his son William whose mother was the daughter of the Earl of Crawford. In the year 1439 the Queen mother married James Stuart son of the Lord of Lorne. This Lord of Lorne's son united himself to the Queen not so much for love as for ambition as he wished to aspire to the government and have the keeping of the young king. Not long after this the King, young though he was took the reins of government into his own hands. One of his first acts was to invite the Douglas to Stirling Castle and there ordered or granted him a "safe conduct". After they had supped the King and Douglas stepped aside and began speaking of the bands then harassing all the country. The King demanded of Douglas that he should withdraw for them, which he refused to do. "Then this shall" said the King, and stabbed him twice with his dagger. This murder caused great commotion among the chiefs of the House of Douglas, but it all ended in the curtailing of their power and the breaking of their authority,

During this period the renowned Wars of the Roses prevented much trouble in Scotland. The Scottish King once crossed the border to help Henry VIth, but it ended in naught. When James was in the South he considered it a fine chance of regaining Berwick and Roxburgh. They began by besieging Roxburgh, and John of the Isles or of Lorne came to assist his sovereign and half brother the King, and was of considerable use in the siege.

This John of Lorne was the son of Sir James Stuart the Black Knight who was the second husband of the Milk White Dove the Queen. She bore three sons to her husband, viz: John, Earl of Athol, James, Earl of Buchan, and Andrew, Bishop of Murray. The eldest John had married by order of the King the celebrated Beatrice, Countess of Douglas. His father Sir James Stuart had died, as well as the King's mother, some time before. He had turned a voluntary exile. The Queen was buried far away from Windsor, where she had first seen her first love, in the Charter House of Perth near her first husband King James, A. D. 1446.

James conducted the siege vigorously and pushed on the operations to such an extent that every thing appeared to portend a speedy end, when the Earl of Huntly arrived with his forces to assist his Sovereign. Dunbar the old Historian thus tells us of his death, "The King with the Earl of Huntly would view the Trenches, and as to welcome a man whose presence seemed to presage good fortune caused discharge a pale of ordinance together; but his coming to this place was as fatal as at Stirling prosperous; for at this salve by the slices of an overcharged piece or wedge the King, his thighbone broken, was stricken immediately dead and the Earl of Angus was sore bruised. This misfortune happened the third of August, the twentyninth or as others, the thirtieth of the King's life; of his reign, twenty-four, the year one thousand four hundred and sixty. James thus died in the flower of his age and was buried in Holyrood Abbey in Edinburgh. His Queen, after the death of her husband arrived at Roxburgh and carried on the siege so vigorously that she took the place and totally destroyed it. The spot where James fell is now marked by a tree in the park of Floors Castle.

CHAPTER X.

CONTENTS:

James III,—The favorite Cochrane.—Sir Andrew Borthwick.—Battle of Sauchie Burn.—The Grey Horse.—Extracts from the Historical Novelist "Grant."

THE King's son at his father's death was only 8 years of age. A quarrel between the Boyds and Kennedys ended in both families being broken. This King when of proper age was married to Margaret, daughter of King Christian of Denmark and Norway on the 6th July 1469. The Islands of Orkney and Shetland were given to the Queen as a dowry and thus from this period they became fixed to the Scottish and English crowns. James as all weak princes, had favorites and they caused him much trouble with the powerful barons of his kingdom. The favorite Cochrane was at last hanged by the confederates which confederacy conspired against the King and resulted in his death at the Battle of Sauchie Burn. We insert though not purely historical, the account of his death from the pen of Scotland's greatest novelist after Sir Walter Scott, viz: "Grant" who in his "*Yellow Frigate*" spiritedly tells of the King's death. However the name of the Borthwick who perpetrated the fatal blow is not Sir Hew, but by Drummond is styled "SIR ANDREW BORTHWICK a Priest" who, "after shrivering" the King "stobb'd him with a dagger."

THE GREY HORSE.

" I would the wind that is sweeping now
   O'er the restless and weary wave;
Were swaying the leaves of the cypress bough
   O'er the calm of my early grave."

Scottish Song.

"The morning of the 11th June, 1488, rose brightly over Stirling and its magnificent scenery.

Almost with dawn, tidings reached King James that the insurgent nobles, at the head of a vast force, had left Falkirk some hours before daybreak, and were on their march through the Torwood to attack him. The unfortunate monarch now found himself peculiarly situated.

His Castle of Stirling, the only adjacent place of security in case of reverse, was closed against him; while the nobles as they marched by the old Roman road which ran through the recesses of the Torwood, barred the only route to the capital. Thus, in the event of defeat, James could turn nowhere for succour but to the admiral's boats at the Craigward, as arranged by the faithful Falconer.

He summoned a council of his chiefs—Montrose, Glencairn, Menteith, Ruthven, Semple, the Preceptor of Torphichen, and others; and they were unanimously of opinion that he should commit their cause and fortunes to the hazard of a battle. Immediately on this decision being come to, the steep streets and old fantastic alleys and wynds of Stirling echoed to the brattle of drums, the clang of trumpets, the twang of Border horns, and the yelling of the mountain pipe, as the royal troops, horse and foot, spearmen, archers, and knights — all sheathed in mail, with horses richly trapped; burgesses and yeomen in splinted jacks, steel gloves, and morions; and clansmen with their long linked lurichs, tuaghs, and two-handed swords, marched past its walls and barrier-ports, by the ancient road, which then, as now, led towards the rampart that extended from the Forth to the Clyde, and advanced eastward in three heavy columns, all animated by enthusiasm for the royal cause, and by the highest spirit and determination.

After hearing mass in the Dominican church, and confessing himself to Henry, Abbot of Cambuskenneth, the king mounted his horse amid a flourish of trumpets. He was a peaceful and amiable prince —one more suited to our own civilized time than that age of blood and cold iron; and thus he felt somewhat unused to the ponderous but gorgeous suit of armour in which he was cased and riveted; and all uncheered by the enthusiasm around him, the flashing of arms, and the braying of martial music, as the drums and fifes, horns and trumpets, of Lord Bothwell's guard (first embodied by James II.), played merrily,

"Cou thou the rashes greene O,"

or by the historical memories of the ground over which he marched, for the Scottish Marathon lay close at hand; he rode silently and moodily on, with his helmet closed, to conceal the tears that came unbidden to his eyes, as he thought of his dead wife, his son's desertion, the unjust accusations against him, and the coming slaughter which nothing but his own death could perhaps avert.

"Another hour will bring us in sight of the foe," said the old Duke of Montrose, whose armour was richly ornamented, though somewhat old-fashioned; for his head-piece had the oreillets and long spike worn in the days of Murdoch, the Regent Duke of Albany, and his horse was gaily housed in his colours; *gules*, a fess checque *argent* and *azure*, the bearings of the Lindsays of Crawford; "and in one hour after that, your majesty will find yourself enabled to punish and repay the treason of Sauchie. I would give my best barony to see his head rolling on the Gowling Hill of Stirling!"

"Time will show, duke," said James, with a sigh. "God wot, I have no wish to shed the blood of my people; but I never liked this Laird of Sauchie; his soul was an abyss, and I never could fathom his thoughts."

"His chief friend and follower—a man named Hew Borthwick—was in Stirling last night, disguised in a friar's frock. This man is a spy and traitor; yet he escaped us, and took the eastern road, doubtless to tell what he has seen; and for all the Howe of Angus, I would not have lost that fellow's head."

"Borthwick! have I not heard that before?"

"Doubtless; he is a well-known bully, pimp, and brawler, who hovers about the discontented lords."

"Is he well-born?"

"Hell-born would be nearer truth, if rumour pedigrees him right," replied Montrose; "but what aileth your majesty?" he asked, perceiving the king to shudder so much that the joints of his armour rattled.

"A *grue* came over me," said the poor king, and Montrose was silent, for neither were above the superstitions of the time; and in Scotland people still believe that an involuntary shudder is caused either by a spirit passing near or when we tread upon the ground which is to be our grave.

A shout, a clamorous hurrah from the vanguard, announced that the foe was in sight; and as the king, with his forces, debouched from the Torwood, he came in view of the long array of his insurgent lords; and Falconer, who rode with the royal guard, shook his lance aloft in fierce ecstacy, as he thought the moment was now approaching when he might meet Hailes and Home, singly or together, in close and mortal combat.

The insurgents were posted at the bridge over the Carron, and were formed in three strong columns, the whole strength of which has been variously stated, for their exact number has never been ascertained. Some historians have estimated them at one hundred and eighty thousand, which is doubless a great exaggeration. Their force, however, was sufficiently formidable to appal the mind of the heart-broken king.

The hostile lines were drawing nearer and more near; the shouts of the wild clansmen of Galloway mingling with the slogans of the Merse-men, who shouted "A Home! a Home!" were borne on the wind across the fertile fields that lay between the approaching columns.

On one side was the poor bewildered king, driven forward with this armed tide, confused, sorrowful, and irresolute, with the royal standard borne over his head by the Constable of Dundee; on the other was the heir of Scotland, agitated also by painful irresolution, by remorse and shame, and also having the royal standard above him, but surrounded by a brilliant band of nobles, all shining in polished steel, gold, plumage, and embroidery; and towards that quarter of the enemy's line, young Ramsay, Lord of Bothwell, at the head of the royal guard, made incredible exertions to hew a passage for the purpose of ridding the king, with his own hand, of as many high-born traitors as possible.

James sat motionless on his magnificent grey charger, with this forest of lances and sea of helmets flashing round him; and not one blow did he strike, but kept his eyes fixed with a species of despair on the banner of his son.

The royal standard was beaten down and its bearer unhorsed; the cannon—the Great Lion—

and all the ensigns were taken, and when the sun of that long summer day was sinking behind the Grampians, and the shadows of the Torwood were deepening on the plain, the king's troop, overborne by numbers, after a long and gallant conflict, gave way, and a total and irreparable rout ensued.

"God help your majesty," said the young Lord Lindsay, as, pale, excited, without a helmet, and with his face streaked by blood, he took the king's horse by the bridle; "the day is lost, yet all is not lost with it while your sacred life is safe. No horse in the field can overtake this grey I gave you. Ride—ride north, and swiftly—the admiral's boats await you at the Craigward—farewell!"

"Ay, farewell, Lindsay — a long farewell to Scotland and to thee—for France or Holland now must be my home."

Thus urged, and knowing that alone and unattended he might escape more easily and unnoticed, than if followed by a train, James turned his grey horse's head towards the north, and gladly left behind that bloody and corpse-encumbered plain.

"And what of the king?" asked several voices.

"The king—is he not on board the *Yellow Frigate?*"

"No," said the admiral; "I would to God he were, for then he would be in safe anchoring ground. Which way did he ride?"

"I know not, for I fell by his side in the middle of the battle——"

"Happy thou, my good Falconer, to share that day's vengeance with the king," said the admiral;

" but that I had other ropes to splice, I had assuredly been with thee. Well?"

All unaware that he was singled out and tracked, James rode from that lost battle-field at a rapid trot, to reach the boats of Sir Andrew Wood; and every sound that rose from the Roman Way and woke the echoes of the Torwood—every shout and random shot of cannon or of hand-gun, made his heart vibrate and leap within him; for even as his own children did this good king love the people of his kingdom.

The coo of the cushat dove, the splashing of the Bannock under its pale green sauch-trees and white-blossomed hawthorns, the rocks spotted with grey lichens and green moss, the flowers, the birds, the foliage, the blue sky, the balmy air, and the beautiful mountains, all spoke to the poor king of his native home and that beloved Scotland which he had now resolved to leave for ever; and as he approached the Bannockburn he leaped the grey charger—Lindsay's last and fatal gift—across from bank to bank, and it cleared them by one furious bound. This was near Beaton's Mill, which still remains about one mile east from the field.

The mill was a strongly-built and old fashioned house with crow-stepped gables, a heavily thatched roof, deep windows obscured by flour; a square ingle-lum, over which the green ivy clustered, stood at one end, while its huge wooden wheel revolved merrily at the other. Its snug and quiet aspect made the king think, with a sigh, (as he shortened his reins and rode on,) how much the contented and unambitious life of the occupant was to be envied.

Now it happened most unfortunately that Mysie Beaton, the gudewife of the Milltoun, was filling a pitcher with water from the dam; and on seeing an armed knight riding at full speed towards her, she uttered a shriek of terror and tossed away the tin vessel, which clattered noisily along the road, while she fled into her cottage adjoining the mill.

Terrified by the rolling pitcher and the foolish woman's sudden cry, the fiery grey horse swerved furiously round and threw his royal rider heavily on the road, close to one of those boor-tree hedges which generally in those days enclosed old gardens and barnyards in Scotland.

While the fatal steed was galloping over the Carse, the miller and his wife raised the body of the inanimate man; and bearing him in, closed the mill-door, carefully secured its tirling-pin, and laid him on their humble box-bed; and then while the kind and sympathizing Mysie busied herself in making up a posset, the miller, her husband, undid the clasps of the gorget and the back and breast-plates, removing them all after taking off the helmet, which he did with ease, as it was opened simply by throwing up the metonniere which guarded the chin and throat, and which turned on the same screw with the vizor.

On doing this the miller saw a pale and handsome face, surrounded by thick, dark clustering hair, and a well-trimmed beard; but the stranger was still senseless, and a streak of blood was flowing from his mouth. On beholding so much manly beauty, the sympathy and remorse of the miller's wife were greatly increased; and on her knees she took the gauntlets off his hands and assisted Gawain to chafe them, and to lave the patient's brow with cool water which he brought from the Bannock in a black leather jack, about sixteen inches high; and then slowly the object of their care began to revive.

"Get me a priest, that I may confess."

"There is none nearer than Cambuskenneth or St. Ninian's Kirk," said Gawain, taking his walking-staff and dagger; "yet I can soon reach either; but may we ask your name, sir?"

"My gudeman, this day, at morn, I was YOUR KING," said James, with a hollow voice and sorrowful emphasis, as he sank back on the coarse box-bed.

Gawain soood as one terrified and confounded on hearing this; but Mysie, his wife, burst into tears, wringing her hands in great fear and excitement, ran out upon the roadway as she heard hoofs approaching.

"A priest," she cried, " a priest, for God's love and sweet St. Mary's sake: a priest to confess the king!"

"To confess whom say ye?" cried the headmost of four armed horsemen, who, with helmets open and swords drawn, galloped up to her in the glooming.

"The king, the king, gude sirs—our puir and sakeless king!"

"And where is he, gudewife?"

"Lying in our puir bed—here, in here, ayont the hallan in my gudeman's mill. Oh, sirs, for a priest!"

"Hush, woman, I am a priest," said the first, who was no other than *Sir* Hew Borthwick, with a glance of infernal import to his three companions, as he leaped from his horse; " lead me to the king."

Borthwick entered the lonely mill, and his three companions, who were no other than Sir Patrick Gray of Kineff, Sir William Stirling of Keir, and Sir James Shaw of Sauchie, after fastening their horses to the hedge without, followed him beyond the *hallan*, or wooden partition which formed the inner apartment."

After a few moments conversation with the king Borthwick stabbed him to the heart and thus died James the 3d of Scotland.

CHAPTER XI.

CONTENTS:

James IVth.—His Iron Belt.—Bell the Cat.—Kilspindie. —Marriage of James with Margaret Tudor.— "The Thistle and the Rose."—Flodden from Sir Walter Scott. —Borthwick the Commander of Artillery.—Flodden by Mackenzie.— Drummond's Flodden.— "News of Battle" by Aytoun.—"The Flowers of the Forest" by Miss Elliott and Do. by Mrs. Cockburn.

"The morn—the marshalling in arms—the day Battle's magnificently stern array." BYRON.

JAMES IVth quietly succeeded his murdered father. Having been in the rebels' army when his father was slain, he felt that he should do some penance for the foul murder of his parent. As such he always wore an iron belt which he is said to have made heavier every succeeding year.

This King delighted in hunting, hawking, racing and all sorts of gaiety. However bearing in mind his father's career he kept on good terms with his nobility. He took them into his counsels and also into his society. Instead of letting them then dwell apart, he invited them to his court and spent the time in gay festivities. He was a free and affable King, and must have possessed no common qualities to manage the fierce and turbulent spirits who surrounded him. It happened one day that the conversation of court turned upon strength and courage. All the courtiers agreed in giving the Earl of Angus, Bell the Cat, the palm of prowess. Spens of Kilspindie however, a great favorite with the King, made some slighting remark. It was true, he said, if Angus was as brave as he was strong.

Some one shortly after told the Earl what he had said. Some time after, Angus, while he was hawking near the Castle of Borthwick, with a single attendant, met Kilspindie. "What reason had ye" said the grim earl, "for making question of my manhood. Thou art a big fellow, and so am I, and one of us shall pay for it." They fought, and the Earl of Angus with a single stroke cut Spens' thigh asunder so that he died on the spot. "Go now," he said to the servant of the slain knight, "tell my gossip, the King, that there was nothing but fair play, I know my gossip will be offended, but I will get me into Liddesdale, and remain in my Castle of Hermitage, till his anger be abated."

After this, the King married the daughter of

Henry VIIth of England by name Margaret Tudor. Lamberton Kirk, three miles from Berwick was the " first kirk in fair Scotland" to receive the bride.

On a beautiful day in mid-summer, several gaily adorned and decorated tents stood pitched beside this little church. A train of Scottish Barons and Lords waited beside the tents. Soon was seen approaching another company, at the head of which was the Earl of Surrey and at his side rode Margaret Tudor, a young and very beautiful girl in the gushing season of maidenhood. With very stately courtesy did the English knight deliver his precious charge into the Scottish barons' care. This fair girl so ceremoniously handed over by the Rose to the Thistle, became a mother and a grand-mother, and the great grand-mother of King James the 6th of Scotland and 1st of England, and thus afterwards were wedded indissolubly in the royal arms of Britain the Thistle and the Rose.

Quarreling with England, James led an army against the enemy and encamped on the field of Flodden. Sir Walter Scott says of James, previous to the battle.

>And why stands Scotland idly now,
>Dark Flodden ! on thy airy brow,
>Since England gains the pass the while
>And struggles through the deep defile ?
>What checks the fiery soul of James ?
>Why sits that champion of the dames
>   Inactive on his steed,
>And sees between him and this land
>Between him and Tweed's southern strand

His host, Lord Surrey, lead ?
What 'vails the vain Knight errant's bran ?
Oh Douglas for thy leading wand !
Fierce Randolph for thy speed !
Oh for one hour of Wallace wight,
Or well skilled Bruce to rule the fight,
And cry, " St. Andrew and our right !"
Another fight had seen that morn,
From fate's dark book a leaf been torn,
And Flodden had been Bannockburn.

The only distinct details of the Battle of Flodden are to be found in Pinkerton's History. When James saw that the English had skilfully gained a position between him and his country he resolved to fight. Burning his tent he descended the hill and the battle began. Surrey moved on and slowly crossed in narrow file, the bridge spanning the river Twisel. Borthwick, the commander of the artillery, earnestly asked permission to cannonade the bridge while the English were crossing.

This *Borthwick* by name *Robert* was the master gunner to the King. He made seven great guns or cannons cast by him, and called *The Seven Sisters* which were taken out of the Castle of Edinburgh and carried to Flodden and placed in position on the Bridge of Twisel. Of this Robert Borthwick commander of King James' artillery, Balfour in his annals A. D. 1509 relates the following—" This zeire, the King entertained one Robert Borthwick, quho foundit and caste maney pices of brasse ordinance of all sisses, in Edinburgh Castle, all of them having this inscription : ' Machina sum Scoto Borthwick fabricata Roberto.'" We cannot say from any authentic record whether this brave soldier and useful artificer died at Flodden or not, or what became of him.

Angus too requested leave to charge before they had time to reform, but both these propositions were rejected by the King. The battle now raged with great fury. The King on foot fought like a hero, and pressed on to meet Surrey till only the length of a lance separated them. Then suddenly the King fell, slain by an arrow and the nobles round him shared the same fate. The King, two prelates, twelve earls, thirteen lords and 10,000 men fell in this fatal battle. But the English also lost heavily, not a man of note save Lord Horne escaped unhurt and Surrey himself declared it was a hard fought fight.

Mackenzie who writes a very popular History of Scotland says: "On that far-away September afternoon, when Surrey met James at the back of Flodden ridge, there were harvest fields waving ripe over broad Scotland, but the strong arms that should have reaped them were stiffening on a bloody heath of a remote border moor. The men of the Lennox and Argyle left their glens and braes, and came to be slaughtered by the men of Lancashire and Cheshire. The men of Caithness, the burghers of St. Johnstone and Dundee, yeomen from the quiet bounds of Fife, and the men of the pleasant dales watered by Southland rivers, rotted in the same heaps with men from the banks of Severn and Thames. Wives wept for these slaughtered husbands and prattling children asked when these dead fathers would return. Two nations ate the bread of tears."

> The English shafts in volleys hail'd,
> In headlong charge their foes assail'd,
> Front, flank and rear, the squadrons sweep
> To break the Scottish circle deep
>   That fought around their King.
> But yet, though thick the shafts as snow,
> Though charging knights like whirlwinds go,
> Though bill-men ply the ghastly blow
>   Unbroken was the ring.
> The stubborn spearmen still made good
> Their dark impenetrable wood,
> Each stepping where his comrade stood·
>   The instant that he fell.
> No thought was there of dastard flight;
> Link'd in the serried phalanx tight,
> Groom fought like noble, squire like knight
>   As fearlessly and well
> Till utter darkness closed her wing,
> On their thin host and wounded King.

SIR WALTER SCOTT.

Nothing can be more definite than the short extract of the Historian Drummond in his researches. He says, A. D. 1681: "The Earl of *Huntly* making down the hill where they encamped near the foot of *Branx Town*, encountreth that wing of the English Host which was led by Sir *Edmund Howard*, after which a furious and long fight he put to flight and so eagerly pursued the advantage that Sir *Edmund* had either been killed or taken, if he had not been rescued by Bastard *Hieron* and the Lord *Dacres*, the battalion which the Earls Lennox and Argyle led (being Highlandmen) encouraged with this glance of victory, loosing their ranks, abandoning all order (for ought that the *French* ambassador *La Motte* by signs, threatening, clamours, could do to them) broke furiously upon the enemy, and invade him the face of whom they are not only valiantly received, but by Sir *Edward Stanley's* traversing the hill, enclosed, cut down at their backs and prostrate. The middle ward which the King led, with which now the Earl of Bothwel with the power of *Lothian* was joined, fought it out courageously body against body and sword against sword. Numbers upon either side falling till darkness, and the black shadows of the night, forced as it were by consent of both, a retreat. Neither of them understanding the fortune of the day and unto whom victory appertained.

Many brave *Scots* did here fall, esteemed to above 5,000, of the noblest and worthest families of the kingdom, who choosed rather to die than outlive their friends and compatriots.

The King's natural son *Alexander* Archbishop of St. Andrews., the Abbots of *Inchjefray* and *Killwinning*, the Earls of *Crawford, Mortoun, Argyle, Lennox, Arrel, Cathness, Bothwel, Athol;* the Lords *Elphinstoun, Areskin, Forbess, Ross, Lovet, Saint Clare, Maxwell* with his three brothers, *Semple* and BORTHWICK ; numbers of gentlemen Balgowny, Blacka—Toure, Borchard, Sir *Alexander Seatoun, Mackenny,* with *Macklean, George,* Master of *Anguss,* and Sir *William Douglass* of *Glenbervy,* with some two hundred gentlemen of their name and vassals were here slain."

A chivalrous and well-known Scottish poet depicts the news of the melancholy event to the inhabitants of Edinburgh. We reproduce the poem here as one of the most spirited lyrics in the English language, and worthy to have fallen from the pen of William Edmonston Aytoun, Editor of *Blackwood's Magazine* and Professor of Rhetoric in Edinburgh University.

>News of battle!—news of battle!
> Hark! 'tis ringing down the street;
>And the archways and the pavement
> Bear the clang of hurrying feet,
>News of battle! who hath brought it?
> News of triumph? Who should bring
>Tidings from our noble army,
> Greeting from our gallant King?
>All last night we watched the beacons
> Blazing on the hills afar,
>Each one bearing, as it kindled,
> Message of the open'd war,
>All night long the northern streamers
> Shot across the trembling sky;
>Fearful lights, that never beacon
> Save when kings or heroes die.
>News of battle! who hath brought it?
> All are thronging to the gate;
>" Warder—warder! open quickly!
> Man—is this a time to wait?"
>And the heavy gates are opened;
> Then a murmur long and loud;

And a cry of fear and wonder
   Bursts from out the bending crowd.
For they see in battered harness
   Only one hard stricken man;
And his weary steed is wounded,
   And his cheek is pale and wan:
Spearless hangs a bloody banner
   In his weak and drooping hand—
What! can that be Randolph Murray,
   Captain of the city band?

Round him crush the people, crying,
   "Tell us all—oh, tell us true!
Where are they who went to battle,
   Randolph Murray, went with you?
Where are they, our brothers—children?
   Have they met the English foe?
Why art thou alone, unfollowed?
   Is it weal or is it woe?"
Like a corpse the grisly warrior,
   Looks from out his helm of steel;
But no word he speaks in answer—
   Only with his armed heel
Chides his weary steed, and onward
   Up the city streets they ride;
Fathers, sisters, mothers, children,
   Shrieking, praying by his side.
"By the God that made thee, Randolph!
   Tell us what mischance hath come."
Then he lifts his riven banner,
   And the asker's voice is dumb.

The elders of the city
   Have met within their hall—

The men whom good King James had charged
   To watch the tower and wall.
"Your hands are weak with age," he said,
   "Your hearts are stout and true;
So bide ye in the Maiden Town,
   While others fight for you.
My trumpet from the Border-side
   Shall send a blast so clear,
That all who wait within the gate
   That stirring sound may hear.
Or, if it be the will of heaven
   That back I never come,
And if, instead of Scottish shouts,
   Ye hear the English drum,—
Then let the warning bells ring out,
   Then gird you to the fray,
Then man the walls like burghers stout,
   And fight while fight you may.
'Twere better that in fiery flame
   The roof should thunder down,
Than that the foot of foreign foe
   Should trample in the town!"

Then in came Randolph Murray,—
   His step was slow and weak,
And, as he doffed his dinted helm,
   The tears ran down his cheek:
They fell upon his corslet,
   And on his mailed hand,
As he gazed around him wistfully,
   Leaning sorely on his brand.
And none who then beheld him
   But straight were smote with fear,

For a bolder and a sterner man
  Had never couched a sprear.
They knew so sad a messenger
  Some ghastly news must bring,
And all of them were fathers,
  And their sons were with the King.

And up then rose the Provost—
  A brave old man was he.
Of ancient name, and knightly fame,
  And chivalrous degree.

Oh, woeful now was the old man's look,
  And he spake right heavily—
" Now, Randolph, tell thy tidings,
  However sharp they be !
Woe is written on thy visage,
  Death is looking from thy face :
Speak ! though it be of overthrow—
  It cannot be disgrace !"
Right bitter was the agony
  That wrung that soldier proud :
Thrice did he strive to answer,
  And thrice he groaned aloud.
Then he gave the riven banner
  To the old man's shaking hand,
Saying—" That is all I bring ye
  From the bravest of the land !
Ay ! ye may look upon it—
  It was guarded well and long,
By your brothers and your children,
  By the valiant and the strong.
One by one they fell around it,
  As the archers laid them low,

Grimly dying, still unconquered,
  With their faces to the foe.
Ay! ye may well look on it—
  There is more than honour there,
Else, be sure, I had not brought it
  From the field of dark despair.
Never yet was royal banner
  Steeped in such a costly dye;
It hath lain upon a bosom
  Where no other shroud shall lie.
Sirs! I charge you keep it holy,
  Keep it, as a sacred thing,
For the stain ye see upon it
  Is the life-blood of your King!"

Woe, woe, and lamentation!
  What a piteous cry was there!
Widows, maidens, mothers, children,
  Shrieking, sobbing in despair!

"O the darkest day for Scotland
  That she ever knew before!
O our King! the good, the noble,
  Shall we see him never more?
Woe to us, and woe to Scotland!
  O our sons, our sons and men!
Surely some have 'scaped the Southron,
  Surely some will come again!"
Till the oak that fell last winter
  Shall uprear its shattered stem—
Wives and mothers of Dunedin—
  Ye may look in vain for them!

Two beautiful Scottish Songs were made on this Battle. "The Flowers of the Forest" were the men of Ettrick dale, who all perished in the fatal fight.

Miss Jane Elliott's version of the song is the following :—

"THE FLOWERS OF THE FOREST."

I've heard a lilting at our ewes' milking,
    Lasses a-lilting before the break o' day;
But now there's a moaning on ilka green loaning,
    The Flowers of the Forest are a' wede away.

At buchts, in the morning, nae blythe lads are scorning;
    The lasses are lonely, and dowie, and wae;
Nae daffing, nae gabbing, but sighing and sabbing;
    Ilk ane lifts her leglen and hies her away.

At e'en in the gloaming nae swankies are roaming
    'Mang stacks, wi' the lasses at bogle to play;
But ilk maid sits drearie, lamenting her dearie—
    The Flowers of the Forest are a' wede away.

In har'st at the shearing nae youths now are jeering;
    The bandsters are runkled, lyart, and grey;
At fair or at preaching, nae wooing, nae fleeching,
    Since our braw foresters are a' wede away.

O dool for the order sent our lads to the border!
    The English for ance by guile wan the day;

The Flowers of the Forest, that aye shone the foremost,
    The prime of the land now lie cauld in the clay.

We'll hear nae mair lilting at the ewes' milking,
    The women and bairns are dowie and wae,
Sighing and moaning on ilka green loaning,
    Since our braw foresters are a' wede away.

Mrs. Cockburn's verses follow :—

"THE FLOWERS OF THE FOREST."

I

I've seen the smiling of fortune beguiling,
    I've felt all its favours, and found its decay;
Sweet was its blessing, kind its caressing,
    But now 'tis fled, 'tis fled far away;
I've seen the forest adorned the foremost,
    With flowers of the fairest, most pleasant and gay,
Sae bonnie was their blooming, their scent the air perfuming,
    But now they are wither'd and are a' wede away.

II

I've seen the morning with gold the hills adorning,
    And the dread tempest roaring before parting day;
        I've seen Tweed's silver streams
            Glitt'ring in the sunny beams,
Grow drumlie and dark as they roll'd on their way.

O fickle fortune why this cruel sporting?
O why thus perplex us, poor sons of a day?
Thy frowns cannot fear me,
Thy smiles cannot cheer me,
For the Flowers of the Forest are withered away.

CHAPTER XII.

CONTENTS.

James V.—Sir David Lindsay.—The King Escapes.— The House of Douglas.—Solway Frith.—Death of the King at Falkland.—Extracts from the "Lady of the Lake."— Don Roderick and Fitz-James.

"She gazed on many a princely port,
Might well have ruled a royal court;
On many a splendid garb she gazed,
Then turned bewildered and amazed,
For all stood bare; and in the room
Fitz-James alone wore cap and plume;
To him each lady's look was lent
On him each courtier's eye was bent;
Midst furs and silks and jewels sheen,
He stood in simple Lincoln green,
The centre of the glittering ring,
And Snowdon's Knight is Scotland's King."

SIR WALTER SCOTT.

AGAIN, at the death of the last King, like the preceding, an infant son, James Vth is left. These minorities of their Kings were of the greatest misfortune to the Scots. Rivals and contending parties were continually embroiling the country north and south, east and west. However in this instance, a thoroughly competent knight was given charge of the youthful monarch, a remarkable man, a famous poet and skilled general, Sir David Lindsay. The first twelve years of the King's life were spent in the society, and under the tutelege of this great man.

Within the year of the late King's death on bloody Flodden field, the Queen bore a posthumous child, and then four months after married the Earl of Angus who was young, handsome and the most powerful of all the Scottish nobility. The Duke of Albany became regent and then quarrelled with Angus whom he banished to France, but he soon returned. The King at 12 years of age was conveyed to Stirling, and William the 4th Lord Borthwick was given the command of it. Drummond says in his History: " Hereupon to preserve the person of the King, he is conveyed from Stirling to the Castle of Edinburgh and trusted to the custody of the Earl of *Marshall*, the Lords *Ruthven* and BORTHWICK two of which should be always resident with him."

Shortly after this the King found himself a prisoner in the hands of the powerful Douglas. He continued in this bondage for two years until he was now sixteen years of age, watching every opportunity of escaping. At last he determined to rid himself of the presence of the hated Douglas. One evening he gave orders to have everything in readiness for a grand hunting the following day. Being to rise very early, the King soon went to bed.

But when the midnight watch was set and all was quiet he slipped out cautiously into the stables. Jockie Hart the groom, saddled horses for three riders, one for the King, another for the King's body-servant and the third for himself. " Now Jockie," said the King, " see that the girths be good and every shoe firm." And then the three set out and through the dark woods of Falkland and out into the open country, with sharp spur and slackened rein did they gallop into Stirling and up its principal street to the Castle, nor stopped they a moment anywhere till they were safe and sound within the bolts and bars of that strong fortress.

The young King now entered on his task of government with a firm hand and with sense and spirit far beyond his years. He insisted on the most determined measures against the Douglas " I vow" he said " that Scotland shall not hold us both" and he kept his word for he was " fain to trot over Tweed," never to return as long as the King lived. James now set himself to redress disorders and " stanch all theft and reaving within his realms" and so assiduously and thoroughly did he carry out his plan that Scotland at last had peace. He had a warm heart and a generous disposition and the people loved to see their King with his face of manly beauty, his piercing blue eyes and yellow hair so affable and free, that still he is called by the soubrequet " The King of the Commons." Quarrelling with his uncle Henry VIIIth of England who wanted to meet him at York,—James was involved in a disastrous war and at the Battle of Solway Frith, his army was utterly routed and he himself retired, crushed by the shameful defeat to Edinburgh. After a few days he went to Falkland. There he would sit for hours brooding over his loss. At last about Christmas he died, just after word had been brought him that his Queen, the celebrated Mary of Guise had born him a daughter. " It will end as it began" he said, "it came with a woman and it will go with a woman." He alluded to the daughter of Robert Bruce by whom the crown of Scotland came into the House of Stuart.

Had he lived till the spring he would have been just thirty-one. He died in the same Castle where fifteen years before he had been a prisoner and from which with Jockie Hart, he had taken his midnight ride. It is clear that James Vth disliked the nobles and endeavored always to break their power. Much of his popularity arose from tales of his free and easy adventures among the peasantry incognito, and not always to his credit or theirs. His personal virtue was little. His mother set him no good example. The imperious and proud Mary of Guise his wife still less, and by this time a flood of profligacy was beginning to sweep over the country.

Though Sir Walter Scott beautifully describes a variety of circumstances in his " Lady of the Lake," nevertheless we must recollect that the Douglas mentioned in that well known poem, is, as the Author himself tells us in his notes appended to the poem, "an imaginary person, a supposed uncle of the Earl of Angus." He also gives interesting stories of the " Gudeman of Ballenguich," as the King styled himself. This history would not be complete without some extracts from the above renowned poem. We give one, the encounter of Don Roderick with Fitz-James. Some beautiful pieces are interspersed throughout this grand poetical effusion amongst which stands "The Boat Song."

> The war pipes ceased; but lake and hill
> Were busy with their echoes still,
> And when they slept, a royal strain
> Bade their hoarse chorus wake again,
> While loud an hundred clansmen raise
> Their voices to their chieftain's praise,
> Each boatman, bending to his oar,
> With measured sweep the burthen bore,
> In such wild cadence, as the breeze
> Makes through December's leafless trees,
> The chorus first could Allan know,
> " Roderigh vich Alpine, ho, iro !"
> And near and nearer as they rowed,
> Distinct the martial ditty flowed.

Next follows the fine scene from Don Roderick in which King James nearly lost his life.

FITZ-JAMES AND DON RODERICK.

The chief in silence strode before,
And reach'd the torrent's sounding shore.
And here his course the chieftain stay'd,
Threw down his target and his plaid,
And to the lowland warrior said :—
" Bold Saxon ! to his promise just,
Vich-Alpine has discharged his trust ;
This murderous chief, this ruthless man,
This head of a rebellious clan,

Hath led thee safe, through watch and ward,
Far past Clan-Alpine's outmost guard.
Now, man to man, and steel to steel,
A chieftain's vengence thou shalt feel.
See, here all vantageless I stand,
Arm'd, like thyself, with single brand;
For this is Coilantogle ford,
And thou must keep thee with thy sword."

The Saxon paused :—"I ne'er delay'd,
When foeman bade me draw my blade;
Nay, more, brave chief, I vow'd thy death;
Yet sure thy fair and generous faith,
And my deep debt for life preserved,
A better meed have well deserved ; .
Can naught but blood our feud atone?
Are there no means?"—"No, stranger, none!
And here,—to fire thy flagging zeal,—
The Saxon cause rests on thy steel;
For thus spoke Fate, by prophet bred
Between the living and the dead:
'Who spills the foremost foeman's life,
His party conquers in the strife.'"

"Then, by my word," the Saxon said,
"The riddle is already read;
Seek yonder brake beneath the cliff,—
There lies Red Murdoch, stark and stiff.
Thus Fate hath solved her prophecy,
Then yield to Fate, and not to me;
To James, at Stirling, let us go,
When, if thou wilt, be still his foe;
Or, if the king shall not agree
To grant thee grace and favor free,

I plight mine honor, oath and word,
That, to thy native strength restored,
With each advantage shalt thou stand
That aids thee now to guard thy land."

Dark lightning flash'd from Roderick's eye—
"Soars thy presumption, then, so high
"Because a wretched kern ye slew,
Homage to name to Roderick Dhu?
He yields not, he, to man nor Fate!
Thou add'st but fuel to my hate.—
My clansman's blood demands revenge!—
  Not yet prepared?—By Heaven I change
My thought, and hold thy valor light,
As that of some vain carpet knight,
Who ill deserved my courteous care,
And whose best boast is but to wear
A braid of his fair lady's hair."

  "I thank thee, Roderick, for the word!
It nerves my heart, it steels my sword;
For I have sworn this braid to stain
In the best blood that warms thy vein.
Now, truce, farewell! and ruth, begone!
Yet think not that by thee alone,
Proud chief! can courtesy be shown.
  Though not from copse, or heath, or cairn,
Start at my whistle clansmen stern,
Of this small horn one feeble blast
Would fearful odds against thee cast;
But fear not—doubt not—which thou wilt,
We try this quarrel hilt to hilt."

  Then each, at once, his falchion drew,
Each on the ground his scabbard threw,

Each look'd to sun, and stream, and plain,
As what they ne'er might see again;
Then, foot, and point, and eye opposed,
In dubious strife they darkly closed.
 Ill fared it then with Roderick Dhu,
That on the field his targe be threw,
Whose brazen studs and tough bull-hide
Had death so often dash'd aside;
For, train'd abroad his arms to wield,
Fitz-James's blade was sword and shield.
 He practised every pass and ward,
To thrust, to strike, to feint, to guard;
While less expert, though stronger far,
The Gael maintain'd unequal war.
Three times in closing strife they stood,
And thrice the Saxon sword drank blood.

 Fierce Roderick felt the fatal drain,
And shower'd his blows like wintery rain,
And, firm as rock, or castle roof,
Against the winter shower is proof,
The foe, invulnerable still,
Foil'd his wild rage by steady skill;
Till, at advantage ta'en, his brand
Forced Roderick's weapon from his hand,
And backwards born upon the lea,
Brought the proud chieftain to his knee.

 " Now yield thee, or, by Him who made
The world, thy heart's blood dyes my blade!"
" Thy threats, thy mercy, I defy!
Let recreant yield who fears to die."
Like adder darting from his coil,
Like wolf that dashes through the toil,

Like mountain-cat who guards her young,
Full at Fitz-James's throat he sprung,
Received, but reck'd not of a wound,
And lock'd his arms his foeman round.

Now, gallant Saxon, hold thine own!
No maiden's hand is round thee thrown!
That desperate grasp thy frame might feel
Through bars of brass and triple steel!
They tug, they strain;—down, down they go,
The Gael above, Fitz-James below.
  The chieftain's gripe his throat compress'd,
His knee was planted on his breast;
His clotted locks he backward threw,
Across his brow his hand he drew,
From blood and mist to clear his sight,
Then gleam'd aloft his dagger bright!
  But hate and fury ill supplied
The stream of life's exhausted tide,
And all too late the advantage came,
To turn the odds of deadly game;
For, while the dagger gleam'd on high,
Reel'd soul and sense, reel'd brain and eye;
Down came the blow! but in the heath
The erring blade found bloodless sheath.
Unwounded from the dreadful close,
But breathless all, Fitz-James arose.

Sir Walter Scott.

CHAPTER XIII.

CONTENTS:

Cardinal Beaton.—Wishart.—John Knox.—Death of Wishart and Beaton. — Sir John Borthwick.— The Galleys. —Mary of Guise.—Siege of Leith.

THE three names which head this chapter are indissolubly connected with the period at which we have arrived in the History of Scotland and previous to the principal events recorded in succeeding chapters especially connected with the life of Mary Queen of Scots. Beaton was a Cardinal and resided at St. Andrew. Wishart had returned to Scotland a short time before the death of James Vth. His description is thus given by a writer of the period, " a tall man, black haired, long bearded with a meek expression of countenance." Independent of all opposition of Cardinal Beaton's, Wishart continued preaching for two years, but when at Dundee, he nearly fell by the hand of a friar who attempted to stab him as he descended from the pulpit, he determined ever after to go armed. He always had carried a two-handed sword before him and that by some true and trusty friends. When he made his last visit to Long Niddry, not far from Edinburgh, the afterwards renowned John Knox who at that time was the tutor to the Douglases of Niddry, carried this sword.

At the town of Haddington when returning to Edinburgh, he was apprehended by the Cardinal's soldiers who carried him to St. Andrew's.

Not many weeks elapsed after this when two events happened there which mark indelibly the Scottish history at this time, the burning of Wishart at the stake and the murder of Beaton by a band of determined men.

Cardinal Bethune or Beaton was one of the greatest persecutors of the Reformed Church. Among those who were so persecuted was SIR JOHN BORTHWICK who was cited before the ecclesiastical court at St. Andrews in 1540 for heresy. Thirteen charges were preferred against him but in particular that he had dispersed heretical books. Sir John fled to England and not appearing when called in court, the charges against him were held as confessed. He was condemned on the 28th May to be burned as a heretic, all his goods and lands were confiscated, his effigy was burned in the market places of St. Andrews and Edinburgh and all men were inhibited from harboring or protecting him. He found a firm protector in the English King Henry VIIIth who received him most graciously and sent him on a mission to the Protestant princes of Germany to concert a confederacy among them in defence of the Reformed religion. After this we hear nothing more of *Sir John Borthwick*.

The murder of Wishart caused the Queen Regent Mary of Guise and the Regent Arran to lay siege to the city of St. Andrews which had now become an asylum for all the destitute and those who opposed the government. John Knox was amongst this number. After three months the plague broke out in the army of the besiegers, and the Regent was obliged to retire. A French fleet however coming to his succour, the brave garrison had to capitulate and they were all sent prisoners to France, Knox and some others being condemned to the galleys as slaves, being instigators and preachers of heresy.

These galleys were long and sharp snouted boats and rowed by from 40 to 50 oars apiece. Cannon grinned from the port-holes of a very strongly built fore castle in the bow of each galley, also from an elevated quarter deck in the stern. These cannon were always loaded and ready for action in case of mutiny. A long, low, undecked middle part of the vessel was packed full of galley slaves, five or six of them chained to each oar. Throughout the whole of the centre of the vessel there ran a gangway on which the drivers or overseers walked and incessantly too, up and down, their terrible whip in hand. The poor miserable slaves never left their benches day or night. "The crack of the whips, the roll and rattle of the oars mingled with the yells of the rowers and the dreadful oaths and curses of the drivers" made it a scene more pandemoniac than human. Alas, that such terrible realities have so often blotted the fair surface of God's earth. A heavy dull sickening smell for ever, day and night, was wafted from this Hell, this charnel house and floated over the horrid den of woe; and as the boat moved on by the united propulsion of the poor wretches' oars, it lingered like the smoke of a steamer's funnel for a long way in the galley's wake. In such a damnable hole, in such a Hell on earth, the mighty Knox for two long years sat chained and rowed on account of his former preaching in St. Andrews and as a heretic and outcast, receiving the lash of the infernal driver, more in spite than for any infringement of galley rule.

Here he waited calmly for the time when God would deliver him and call him once again to preach His Holy Gospel in his native land. At last he was liberated from the galley, but still he is a wanderer on the face of the earth, sometimes at Berwick, then at Newcastle, again at London then in Scotland and throughout the Continent especially at Frankfort and Geneva.

At this time Mary of Guise took the reins of government into her own hands and so thoroughly discontented had the people become, that when a few and bold men were summoned to appear before her for preaching they did so but great numbers of their friends, armed, came with them. Some of these gentlemen even made their way to the Queen's chamber and threatened that they would suffer it no longer. At this time they recalled John Knox and signed the "Solemn League and Covenant." At Perth the Lords of the Congregation began their reformation. A civil war ensued but they were backed by Queen Elizabeth of England, whilst the Queen Regent was assisted by a French fleet one of her most powerful friends was John, Fifth Lord Borthwick son of the Lord slain in Flodden. Leith was besieged and great atrocities were committed. The French stripped the bodies of their enemies naked and laid them in rows along the ramparts of the town. The Queen Mother from the heights of Edinburgh Castle saw the sight and danced for joy, "yonder," she said "is the fairest tapestry that I ever saw. I would the whole fields betwixt me and them were strowed with the same stuff." The French at last had to surrender to the Lords of the Congregation and were shipped off to their own country and thus after many years of trouble, bloodshed and intrigue, the friends of civil and religious liberty now hoped that peace and prosperity would settle on Scotland.

CHAPTER XIV.

CONTENTS:

Queen Mary.—Her Birth.—Stay at Linlithgow.—Coronation. — The Five Marys.— Sent to France.— Arrival.— Life at St. Germain's.—The Convent.— Life in France.

> " Yestreen the Queen had foure Maries,
> This nicht she'll hae but three,
> There was Mary Beton and Mary Seton
> And Mary Livingston an' me."—
> Old Song.

WE have now arrived at the principal period of this History. We enter on the career of Queen Mary, the first and last of the Scottish Queens who reigned in her own right and like Elizabeth and our present most gracious Majesty Victoria, alone. We have seen that when her father James Vth lay dying in the Castle of Falkland of a broken heart on account of his defeat at Solway Firth, news of the birth of a child arrived. The post from Linlithgow brought him the intelligence that the Queen was the mother of a child. He enquired whether it were a boy or a girl and the messenger answered :

"It is a fair daughter," when the King answered, according to another chronicler "Adieu, farewell, it came with a lass and it will pass with a lass," and so recommending himself to Almighty God, he turned his face to the wall and almost afterwards died.

Let us pass over the space of nine months during which time nothing but intrigue and bitter jealousies prevailed over the unconscious infant. Henry the Bluff of England urged his claims not only energetically but imperiously and being met by the stern veto of the Scottish peers, modified his requests and asked only that the Queen be given up to him and sent to England till she were 10 years of age and then that she espouse the young Prince of Wales. On the 1st of July 1543, a treaty was concluded between Bluff Henry and the Scottish Regent. During all this excitement the unconscious Scottish Queen was smiling in helpless infancy in the strong Castle of Linlithgow. Beneath her cradle in all its glory, dazzling from the noonday sun, sparkled the waters of beautiful Loch Leven, showers of diamonds were sent forth from the lovely fountains, and Janet her nurse, was far more welcome than all the salutations of all the iron and steel clad warriors, earls or barons who came to look upon the child and to congratulate Mary of Guise, the widowed mother.

It was then determined to crown the infant on the 9th of September 1543 at Stirling Castle, where in days of yore the Kings of Scotland had been crowned. This day was one of universal and thrilling interest throughout all the land. Scotland had never before seen a female in her own right crowned Queen. She was the first female sovereign on the throne of the great Robert Bruce who was to be invested with crown and sceptre. France and England two great rival powers and all the Reformers of Europe looked on with feelings each according to their own desire. From Orkney and Caithness, from Inverness and the Isles, from Argyll and the land of Buchan, from Galloway and Clyde, from Berwick and Borthwick, from the Pentland Hills and the Ochills, from Cape Wrath to Burrough Head, all classes pressed on to see the grand and mighty spectacle. Winding up the steep ascents of Stirling might be seen Highland and Lowland, English and French. Up, up, they go to the battlements of the grand old castle, and now the trumpets bray, the music waxes louder and louder. See in that glittering train appears the infant Queen and then the Earl of Arran who bears the crown, whilst Lennox follows immediately after, carrying the sceptre. The Cardinal of St. Andrews placed the crown on the infant brow and the tremendous shout, "Long live the Queen" shook the old Rock of Stirling to its very base. But little dreamt that smiling babe of the troublous life before her.

Soon after this and less than six months after Henry's treaty it was annulled and an alliance with France was signed at Edinburgh by the Regent of Scotland which occasioned war with England. The enraged Henry VIIIth laid waste a large portion of Scotland, but the Scots received auxiliary troops from France and what we have mentioned in a former chapter took place. During all this period of between five and six years, Mary passed her life at Stirling Castle and here the news of the defeat of Pinkie reached the royal ears. As Stirling was in danger of assault Mary was removed to Inchmahome Island, to the monastery there, where sheltered by its isolation she was thought to be secure from English foe. During her residence here her mother Mary of Guise and Lady Fleming, daughter of James IVth, her governess, formed a social class of four young girls of her own age who were her constant companions for many years after. Their names were Mary Beaton, Mary Fleming, Mary Livingston and Mary Seaton. Very little is known of Queen Mary's life at Inchmahome. She was next removed to Dumbarton Castle on the banks of the River Clyde, but very soon after sent to France. After a pleasant voyage the five Marys arrived safely at Brest 13th August 1548. She was received with great pomp by the King of France and the gorgeous procession moved on towards Paris in one grand extravagance of pomp, well described by French historians of the period. Convicts received their pardon, prison doors flew open and joyous exultation pervaded all classes. This was indeed a strange and exciting scene to the laughing girl and her companions who beheld the whole.

After a brief residence at the celebrated palace of St. Germains, the young Queen was received into a Convent where she lived surrounded by the devotional exercises and ascetic humiliations of the community within its walls. The King hearing that she was most piously inclined demanded that she should be transferred to his palace, which was done. This was not the best place of training which the Queen could get and totally different from the pious and quiet life of the Convent which she had left. The court of the French King at this time was one of the utmost magnificence, elegance and joy but we must add one of the most lax in all Europe. The days passed in a half-chivalric and half-literary occupation. Francis I, the French King and father of Henry II, had collected into his court and retinue all the principal nobility of France. He had as pages scions of all the chief families in the land and nearly two hundred young ladies lended splendour to his court. It thus descended to his son who succeeded. The palaces of Fontainbleau and St. Germains, and the Castles of Blois and Amboise were all one scene of grandeur and magnificence and in the writings of an Historian of the period, "There was a host of human goddesses, some more beautiful than others; every lord and gentleman conversed with her he loved best; whilst the King talked to the Queen, the Dauphiness (Mary Stuart) and the Princesses together with these Lords and Ladies and Princes who were seated nearest him." Mary's education did not profit well amidst all this elaborate culture and pageantry, and during the few years of this incessant round of gaiety and pleasure little did she think of that stern land which had cradled her. When about eight years old her mother reached Rouen in France. After a dazzling reception by the French monarch and his attendants she was admitted into the presence of her daughter. So beautiful had the young Queen grown that it is said the Queen Dowager shed tears of joy at the sight. For a whole year, Mary enjoyed the society of her gifted mother, but at last the parting took place and they never after met again on this side of Eternity. When she was eleven her out door amusements were chiefly hawking and hunting. On one occasion, when she was riding at full speed in pursuit of a stag and whilst attended by a brilliant company of courtiers and nobility, her dress accidentally caught in the bough of a tree and instantly she was thrown from her palfrey to the ground. The whole company halted in amazement and terror but Mary making no outcry, arranged her disheveled hair, remounted again and once more dashed off and forward in the chase.

CHAPTER XV.

CONTENTS:

Francis II.—The Dauphin.— Interview of Francis and Mary. — Betrothal. — The Marriage. — Miss Benger's Translation of Buchanan's description of Queen Mary.

"The kirk was deck'd at morning tide,
The tapers glimmer'd fair
The priest and bridegroom wait the bride,
And dame and knight were there."
SCOTT.

"Like harmony her motion,
  Her pretty ankle is a spy,
Betraying fair proportion
  Wad mak' a saint forget the sky,
Sae warming, sae charming
  Her faultless form and gracefu' air,
Ilk feature—auld nature
  Declared that she could do nae mair."
BURNS.

FRANCIS II of France, the first of the suitors and Mary's first husband, was the son of Henry II and his wife Catherine de Medicis. He was born at Fontainbleau 19th January 1544, and he therefore was just a year younger than the fair Queen of Scots. When they were both in their youngest years they had been set apart as just the pair to match and cement the two kingdoms over which each was to reign. This attachment began in the earliest days of Mary's life in France. When she was about ten years of age, the Dauphin nine, one day meeting in the beautifully terraced gardens of Fontainbleau, the shy and timid boy was about to pass the bevy of the fair beautiful virgins with only the polite recognition of acquaintance, though his heart beat high even then for the fairest of the five. "François mon ami," why pass us all so politely? Come, let us walk through these beautiful grounds, says Mary Stuart.

"Delighted will I be to accompany thee, oh fair goddess, for nothing will give me greater pleasure than by showing you all the beauties of this wonderful place."

"Come, then, for I know Lady Fleming will let us enjoy ourselves on this glorious day and amongst these old majestic oaks."

So saying the youthful six accompanied by their tutor and governess rambled away amongst the alcoves and arcades covered with vines laden with their luscious fruit, till, stopping at the end of one of these avenues where a famous vine tempted them with many large clusters of grapes, Francis pulled one bunch and handing it gracefully to the youthful Queen said. "Accept this from you betrothed, let me hear that you look not carelessly upon me, and I shall be happy."

"Mia cara sposa," replied the Queen. She said no more, but blushing ran quickly away and overtook the other girls.

From this time it was tacitly understood between them that, what their parents intended should by themselves be carried out. Year after year passed and saw Mary grow beautiful and more beautiful and her mind kept advancing at the same time, as she became a good linguist, and French, Spanish and English with the dead languages were all mastered, with those accomplishments which belonged to that polite and refined court. During this period the health of Francis was very bad. He was constitutionally as well as mentally weak, but he was amiable and when roused from his lethargy, energetic. Timid and shrinking from responsibilities, the King his father and others arranged the nuptials of the pair. They were appointed to be celebrated on the 24th April 1558.

Previous to this, at the signing of the deeds and papers of betrothment, the King requested that she, Queen Mary would sign the document he held in his hand.

"And what is the import of its contents, my liege" replies Mary.

"It is that a full and free donation of the kingdom of Scotland be henceforth given and for ever, to the Kings of France."

"But my liege Lord how can I do this when the Dauphin and I have promised to the Scottish Commissioners to preserve, as the paper we signed says "the integrity of the kingdom and observe its ancient laws and liberties."

"Easily enough," replied the King, frowning a little and looking Mary steadily in the face. "Easily enough," when the Dauphin is King of France and Scotland and you are Queen of France and Scotland you can easily accede to the terms of the Scottish document."

"C'est bien," replied the Queen and without further colloquy she affixed her sign and wrote her name in a clear and bold hand.

"Now this is as a dutiful daughter-in-law should do." King Henry said, for continued he. "You know that during all the years of your minority I have maintained the independence of Scotland against the English her ancient and inveterate enemies and my protecting hand shall ever be held over her."

Laying the signed paper down, the King drew from a portfolio lying on the table where the marriage documents were, another and larger parchment sheet and again requested Mary to sign. Turning to the Duke of Guise and the Cardinal of Lorraine her two uncles who were present, she asked them what she should do.

"May it please your Majesty," said the Cardinal "will you tell my niece what are the principal items transcribed thereon so that she may know what she signs and the purport thereof."

"Certainly" replied the King, "and I thank my Lord Cardinal, that his training has such effect on so beauteous and enlightened a subject, and now my beloved daughter this second deed is only a repetition as it were of the first, in case of its failure. The usufruct of the kingdom of Scotland is by this deed granted to the King of France, until he shall be repaid the sums which he has expended in the defence of Scotland. We estimate these expenses at one million pieces of eight and only wish the mortgage to remain until this sum be paid."

" My Liege Lord the King, as I have signed the first I am ready to sign the second" and she again affixed her name. Then followed the signatures of the marriage documents and papers.

All Paris was now alive with the preparations for this long looked for event. These papers were signed on the 19th April and on the 24th the nuptials were to take place. As the 19th was her betrothment in conformity to the usual custom, they were privately signed in the great hall of the Louvre, and a magnificent ball given in the evening. Between the palace of the Bishop and the great Church of Notre Dame a covered gallery was erected so that the spectators might see the royal procession as it moved along. This gallery was lined with purple velvet and embossed with rich, costly and elaborate ornamentation and at the Cathedral opened up at both sides into an amphitheatre of vast proportions, reminding one of those of ancient Rome.

At last the 24th of April arrived and it happened to be a Sunday. Throngs of gaily dressed and excited people were seen hastening from all quarters to the great covered area, to witness the magnificent pageantry which on account of the honor of the event was called the Triumph. Right over the grand entrance of Notre Dame, a royal canopy strewn with *Fleurs de lis* and around stood the principal Churchmen, as the Papal Legate, the Archbishops and Bishops, all in their sacerdotal robes. Bands of music everywhere struck the ears with Swiss melodies.

First came the Duke of Guise as the grand marshall and master of the King's household. Saluting with courtly dignity, all these great men of the Church and perceiving that the people could not well see for the large number of these grandees, he requested that they might enter the Cathedral porch and allow the assembled crowd to view the procession. And now rolls on the bridal music, trumpet and lute, bass-viol and flageolet, violin and hautboy all intermingle in harmonious concert, then follow two hundred gentlemen attached to the person of the King, next come the Princes of the royal blood and their attendants, then follow Bishops and Abbots with their croziers and mitres borne before them, then a cluster of high-capped cardinals, conspicuous among whom was seen John of Bourbon, Charles of Lorraine and John of Guise, after them came the Legate of the Pope, borne before whom was a magnificent and massive cross of gold, next came the Dauphin Francis conducted by the King of Navarre. Although poor Francis looked feeble, and was naturally ill-proportioned yet no one envied the fine look of his younger brothers, the Duke of Orleans and Angouleme as Francis was the important personage in this day's programme. Great was the sensation when the beautiful Mary, the fair and youthful bride appeared, supported by her father-in-law the King of France and her young kinsman the Duke of Lorraine. Although scarcely yet sixteen years of age, she was tall and stately, and so perfect was the beautiful symmetry of her form and so graceful in all her movements that every eye followed her every motion and she appeared as Brantome the Historian describes her " more beautiful and charming than a celestial Goddess; for as every eye dwelt with rapture on her face, every voice echoed her praise; whilst universally in the court and city it was re-echoed, "happy, thrice happy, the prince who should call her his, even though she should have had neither crown nor sceptre to bestow." Her train long and sweeping was borne by two beautiful young girls, her neck was encircled by a diamond carcanet from which depended a ring of immense value. She wore on her head a coronet of gold, surrounded with precious stones, conspicuous amongst which were seen the diamond, ruby and emerald, and in the centre shone a carbuncle valued at 500 crowns. Immediately behind the youthful Queen came Catherine de Medicis and the Prince de Conde, Marguerite, the Queen of Navarre and a long train of distinguished ladies.

As soon as the procession reached the main entrance of the Cathedral of Notre Dame, the King drew off from his finger a ring, which he gave to the Archbishop of Rouen who placing it on Queen Mary's finger, at once pronounced the nuptial benediction. Then followed mutual congratulations and the lovely Queen saluting her husband, called him the King of Scots. The Archbishop of Paris then delivered a discourse and when concluded, the herald began to shower money among the people, which occasioned a great deal of confusion. Then the royal pair advanced to the choir and mass was celebrated. Afterwards a costly collation and a ball were given in the Bishop's palace. Early in the evening, the royal pair and the King of France returned to their palace. So remarkable were the festivities of this night that we give an extract from one of the chroniclers of the day. "While the guests were becoming animated with pleasure twelve artificial horses mantled in golden cloth, entered with the motion of life and bestrode by sons of the nobility. Next came a company of pilgrims each reciting a poem; then were ushered into the hall six very small galleys, and as the historian states—" Covered like Cleopatra's barge with cloth of gold and crimson velvet; so skilfully contrived as to appear to glide through the waves, sometimes rolling, sometimes backing then veering as if agitated by a sudden swell of the tide, till the delicate silken sails were cracked asunder." On the deck of each diminutive vessel sat a cavalier, who, whilst the navy moved along sprang in turn to the land and seized a fair and beauteous lady bearing her away in triumph to his vessel to a vacant chair ready for her reception. For no less than fifteen days did these extravagancies last till all were almost satiated with the variety of the scenes.

A celebrated English writer Miss Benger has given us in the following translation of Buchanan a poet of this period, an idea of the beauty and grace of the Scottish Queen.

"For say, if met as once on Ida's height,
The assembled Gods had held their awful state;
Heard thy young vow and to thy prayer had given
In wedded love, the choisest born of Heaven,
What brighter form could meet thy ravished sight
Or fill thy bosom with its pure delight?
On her fair brow a regal grace she wears,
While youth's own lustre on her cheek appears,
And soft the rays from those bright eyes that gleam
Whose temper'd light and chasten'd radiance seem
As thought mature had given the beams of truth
Gently to mingle with the fire of youth."

CHAPTER XVI.

CONTENTS:

Description of the Scottish Nation by Buchanan.—Title of Francis and Mary.—Death of Francis.—The Queen's Mourning Seal.— Preparation to return to Scotland. — Leaving France. — Adieu. — Bell's "Mary Queen of Scots."

"My former hopes are dead,
My terror now begins. COWPER.

"Et, longum formosa vale, vale, inquit, Iola."

"In freta dum fluvii current, dum montibus umbræ,
Lustrabunt convexa, polus dum sidera pascet;
Semper honos, nomenque tuum, laudesque manebunt.
Quæ me cunque vocant terræ."
VIRGIL'S ÆNEID.

WE will give one other extract, this time in praise of the Scottish people, whom Queen Mary, though educated in France, did not undervalue :—

" I will not tell of Scotia's fertile shores,
Or mountain tracts that teem with choisest ores,
Or living streams from sources rich, that flow,
For other regions natures' bounties show—
(And thirst of wealth alone their souls employ,
Whose grovelling spirits feel no loftier joy.)
But this her own, and this her proudest fame
The strength, the virtue of her sons to claim,
'Tis theirs in early chase to rouse the wood,
And fearless theirs to breast the foaming flood,
Their swords her bulwark and their breasts her
 shield ;
'Tis theirs to prize pure fame e'en life above,
Firmly their faith to keep, their God to love,
And while stern war its banner wide unfurl'd
Terror and change o'er half the nations hurl'd ;
This the proud charter that in ages gone,
Saved their lov'd freedom and its ancient throne."

By the return of the Scots Commissioners to Scotland the title which was bestowed on the young King and Queen, was " Francis and Mary, King and Queen of Scotland, Dauphin and Dauphiness of Vienne" and hereafter in all Parliamentary Acts the above title was the signature at the end.

The Dauphin's father Henry had been accidentally mortally wounded by Count Montgommeri at a tournament and died eleven days after, 10th July 1359. Francis was confined to his couch in the palace of Versailles when the officers of state entered his apartment and announced his father's death, on the bended knee of loyalty, by saluting him King. " As if, writes one relating the circumstance," an earthly voice had sent the health—thrill along his nerves, he sprang from his bed and declared he was well. Scarcely had Francis conferred with his counsellors, before his mother joined them, to accompany him to the Louvre, where would be offered the usual congratulations and homage, upon the transfer of a crown to the brow of a successor. Mary silently followed in the train, when Catherine, who saw the declining glory of her family, in the elevation of the Guises, said to her, " Pass on Madam, it is now for you to take precedence." The young Queen acknowledged the civility but on reaching the chariot refused to enter, until the desponding and ambitious widow passed in before her. The Dauphin was then crowned at Rheims, where that ceremony had long been performed and immediately assumed the reins of government." But the delicate young King was only a tool in the hands of these ambitious men Cleric and Lay who were about the throne.

For a short period in a quiet country seat near Paris the youthful pair lived and loved each other dearly. The health of Francis however never good, shortly after his marriage began to fail, and the Guises always imperious, ruled him with a rod of iron. One day the poor delicate King suddenly fainted and was borne by his attendants, Mary loudly lamenting at his side to his private chamber, only to die. Faithfully did the beautiful young Queen attend by his bedside, and every act of kindness and of soothing comfort were received with the gratitude of a child by the dying King. But no human power could arrest the summons of death, the King of Terrors, all the best physicians of the time gave their consultation but of no avail. Rapidly sinking the youthful King expired on the 5th December 1560. By his death Scotland and France once more became disunited and the lovely Queen retired to seclusion in the palace. Here she gave herself up to grief and solitude and invented a mourning seal, viz: A liquorice tree, whose root is the valuable part and beneath the motto " DULCE MEUM TERRA TEGIT." " *My treasure is in the ground.*" After visiting her relations, by the force of circumstances she was obliged to declare that she must return to Scotland. When it finally was settled that the Queen was to return, Catherine's proud spirit relented somewhat towards the youthful Queen. She accompanied Mary to St. Germains where thirteen years previously she had first seen and embraced the beautiful laughing girl. In a triumphal procession the departing Queen made her journey from St. Germains to Calais. She had to remain for six days at Calais before she saw the ship ready to take her back to her native land. Her four Marys were with her still, and amidst tears and lamentations she embarked on board her vessel. Her mind was naturally superstitious, and Brantome writing of this occasion and he was one of her attendants, says: " Habitually superstitious, in embarking for the royal galley, Mary was appalled by the mournful spectacle of a vessel striking against the pier, and sinking to rise no more;—overwhelmed with the sight, the unhappy Queen exclaimed: "O God! what fatal omen is this for a voyage!" then rushing towards the stern she knelt down, and covering her face sobbed aloud "Farewell! France, farewell! I shall never, never see thee more!"

The galley having left port soon set sail. She with both arms resting on the poop of the galley near the helm, began to shed floods of tears, continually casting her beautiful eyes towards the port and the country she had left and uttering these mournful words: "Farewell, France"! until night began to fall. She desired to go to bed without taking any food and would not go down to her cabin, so her bed was prepared on deck. She commanded the steersman, as soon as it was day, if he could still discern the coast of France, to wake her and fear not to call her, in which fortune favored her; for, the wind having ceased and recourse being had to the oars, very little progress was made during the night; so that when day appeared, the coast of France was still visible and the steersman, not having failed to perform the commands which she had given to him, she sat up in her bed, and began again to look at France as long as she could, and then she redoubled her lamentations; "Farewell, France! Farewell, France! I shall never see thee more." She wrote the following beautiful poem on this occasion:—

ADIEU.

"Adieu, plaisant pays de France,
O ma patrie,
La plus chérie;
Qui a nourri ma jeune enfance,

Adieu, France, adieu, mes beaux jours !
La nef qui déjoint mes amours,
N'a ici de moi que la moitié
Une perte te reste ; elle est tienne ;
Je la fis à ton amitié,
Pour que de l'autre il te souvienne."

We must insert here that beautiful poem, by Bell, on the occasion of Queen Mary leaving France. Though it carries on the thread of our History to its close, nevertheless it will always repay the perusal, wherever it is found.

MARY QUEEN OF SCOTS.

I look'd far back into other years, and lo ! in bright array
I saw, as in a dream, the forms of ages pass'd away.
It was a stately convent, with its old and lofty walls,
And gardens with their broad green walks, where soft the footstep falls,
And o'er the antique dial-stones the creeping shadow pass'd,
And all around the noon-day sun a drowsy radiance cast.
No sound of busy life was heard, save from the cloister dim
The tinkling of the silver bell, or the sisters' holy hymn.
And there five noble maidens sat beneath the orchard trees,
In that first budding spring of youth, when all its prospects please ;

And little reck'd they, when they sang, or knelt at
  vesper prayers,
That Scotland knew no prouder names—held none
  more dear than theirs :—
And little even the loveliest thought, before the
  holy shrine,
Of royal blood and high descent from the ancient
  Stuart line :
Calmly her happy days flew on, uncounted in their
  fight,
And as they flew, they left behind a long-continu-
  ing light.

The scene was changed. It was the court, the gay
  court of Bourbon,
And 'neath a thousand silver lamps a thousand
  courtiers throng :
And proudly kindles Henry's eye—well pleased, I
  ween, to see
The land assemble all its wealth of grace and chivalry :—
But fairer far than all the rest who bask on fortune's tide,
Effulgent in the light of youth, is she, the new-
  made bride !
The homage of a thousand hearts—the fond deep
  love of one—
The hopes that dance around a life whose charms
  are but begun,—
They lighten up her chestnut eye, they mantle o'er
  her cheek,
They sparkle on her open brow, and high-soul'd
  joy bespeak :

Ah! who shall blame, if scarce that day, through all its brilliant hours,
She thought of that quiet convent's calm, its sunshine and its flowers?

The scene was changed. It was a bark that slowly held its way,
And o'er the lee the coast of France in the light of evening lay;
And on its deck a lady sat, who gazed with tearful eyes
Upon the fast-receding hills, that dim and distant rise.
No marvel that the lady wept,—there was no land on earth
She loved like that dear land, though she owed it not her birth;
It was her mother's land, the land of childhood and of friends,—
It was the land where she had found for all her griefs amends,—
The land where her dead husband slept—the land where she had known
The tranquil convent's hush'd repose, and the splendors of a throne;
No marvel that the lady wept,—it was the land of France—
The chosen home of chivalry—the garden of romance!
The past was bright, like those dear hills so far behind her bark;
The future, like the gathering night, was ominous and dark!

One gaze again—one long, last gaze—" Adieu, fair
   France, to thee!"
The breeze comes forth—she is alone on the un-
   conscious sea!

The scene was changed. It was an eve of raw and
   surly mood,
And in a turret-chamber high of ancient Holyrood
Sat Mary, listening to the rain, and sighing with
   the winds
That seem'd to suit the stormy state of men's un-
   certain minds.
The touch of care had blanch'd her cheek—her
   smile was sadder now,
The weight of royalty had press'd too heavy on her
   brow;
And traitors to her councils came, and rebels to the
   field;
The Stuart *sceptre* well she sway'd, but the *sword*
   she could not wield.
She thought of all her blighted hopes—the dreams
   of youth's brief day,
And summoned Rizzio with his lute, and bade the
   minstrel play
The songs she loved in early years—the songs of
   gay Navarre,
The songs perchance that erst were sung by gallant
   Chatelar;
They half beguiled her of her cares, they soothed
   her into smiles,
They won her thoughts from bigots zeal and fierce
   domestic broils:—
But hark! the tramp of armed men! the Douglas'
   battle-cry!

They come—they come!—and lo! the scowl of
    Ruthven's hollow eye!
And swords are drawn, and daggers gleam, and
    tears and words are vain—
The ruffian steel is in his heart—the faithful Rizzio's slain!
Then Mary Stuart dash'd aside the tears that trickling fell:
"Now for my father's arms!" she said; "my woman's heart farewell!"

The scene was changed. It was a lake, with one
    small lonely isle,
And there, within the prison walls of its baronial
    pile,
Stern men stood menacing their queen, till she
    should stoop to sign
The traitorous scroll that snatch'd the crown from
    her ancestral line:—
"My lords, my lords!" the captive said, "were I
    but once more free,
With ten good knights on yonder shore to aid my
    cause and me,
That parchment would I scatter wide to every
    breeze that blows,
And once more reign a Stuart-queen o'er my remorseless foes!"
A red spot burn'd upon her cheek—stream'd her
    rich tresses down,
She wrote the words—she stood erect—a queen
    without a crown!

The scene was chang-d. A royal host a royal banner bore,
And the faithful of the land stood round their smiling queen once more :—
She stay'd her steed upon a hill—she saw them marching by—
She heard their shouts—she read success in every flashing eye.
The tumult of the strife begins—it roars—it dies away;
And Mary's troops and banners now, and courtiers —where are they?
Scatter'd and strewn and flying far, defenceless and undone;—
Alas! to think what she has lost, and all that guilt has won!
Away! away! thy gallant steed must act no laggard's part;
Yet vain his speed—for thou dost bear the arrow in thy heart!

The scene was changed. Beside the block a sullen headsman stood,
And gleam'd the broad axe in his hand, that soon must drip with blood.
With slow and steady step there came a lady through the hall,
And breathless silence chain'd the lips and touch'd the hearts of all.
I knew that queenly form again, though blighted was its bloom,
I saw that grief had deck'd it out—an offering for tomb!

I knew the eye, though faint its light, that once so brightly shone;
I knew the voice, though feeble now, that thrill'd with every tone;
I knew the ringlets, almost gray, once threads of living gold!
I knew that bounding grace of step—that symmetry of mould!
E'en now I see her far away, in that calm convent aisle,
I hear her chant her vesper hymn, I mark her holy smile;
E'en now I see her bursting forth upon the bridal morn,
A new star in the firmament, to light and glory born!
Alas! the change!—she placed her foot upon a triple throne,
And on the scaffold now she stands—beside the block—*alone!*
The little dog that licks her hand—the last of all the crowd
Who sunn'd themselves beneath her glance, and round her footsteps bow'd;
Her neck is bared—the blow is struck—the soul is pass'd away!
The bright—the bautiful—is now a bleeding piece of clay!
The dog is moaning piteously; and, as it gurgles o'er,
Laps the warm blood that trickling runs unheeded to the floor!
The blood of beauty, wealth, and power—the heart-blood of a queen,—

The noblest of the Stuart race—the fairest earth
    has seen,—
Lapp'd by a dog! Go, think of it, in silence and
    alone;
Then weigh against a grain of sand the glories of a
    throne!

CHAPTER XVII.

CONTENTS:

Mary's return to Scotland.—Arrival at Leith.—The Queen and her Reception.—Holyrood.—Lord James Stuart.—The Queen at the head of her Army.—The Queen in the Parliament House.

> " A weary lot is thine, fair maid
> A weary lot is thine!
> To pull the thorn thy brow to braid
> And press the rue for wine!
>
> SIR WALTER SCOTT.

AFTER a wearisome and saddened night when the morning dawned, the tears of the Queen flowed again at the sight of the thin line of distant horizon which she knew was France she was leaving for ever. A soft breeze in the meanwhile springing up, caused them to proceed more rapidly than they had during the night. This breeze filled the drooping sails and gently lifted the Queen's beautiful tresses and then the rowers ceased the monotonous measured strokes and the galley was driving onwards by the now increasing breeze. Whilst bravely cutting the waters, the vessel swept suddenly past a dangerous shoal, now no more and

Mary remarked to her attendants, on the peril to which they had been exposed, " that for the sake of her friends and for the common weal she ought to rejoice, but that for herself she should have esteemed it a privilege so to have ended her course." And so speeds on the royal Galley and now Berwick is passed, that town which lies between the contending countries, that town which witnessed the death blow of Edward IInd, when he arrived there after the decisive victory of Bannockburn. Sailing on they pass in the distance, Dunbar. Little does the beautiful young Queen know of the part she will yet play at that Castle of Bothwell. Sweeping round North Berwick Head they enter the Firth of Forth and safely passing Inchkeith, sailed into the harbour of Leith on the 19th day of August 1561.

A very heavy fog had settled over the Firth and on account of this, her arrival was expected to be somewhat delayed, but the tidings flew like wild fire or those Highland couriers when they carried the fiery cross, and the people flocked in crowds to welcome their youthful Queen and to behold her beauty which enchanted them all, though fearful of that religion which she had brought with her.

Here we will give a graphic description of the Queen and her reception from the pen of Scotland's great Reformer John Knox. He says : " The very face of the heavens at the time of her arrival did manifestly speak what comfort was brought into this country with her, to wit : sorrow, dolour, darkness and all impiety ; for in the memory of man that day of the year was never seen a more dolorous face of the heavens, than was at her arrival which two days after did so continue; for, besides the surface wet, and the corruption of the air, the mist was so thick and dark that scarce could any man espy another the length of two pair of butts. The sun was not seen to shine two days before nor two days after. That forewarning, gave God to us, but alas! the most part were blind.

"At the sound of the cannon which the galleys shot, happy was he or she that first must have presence of the Queen. The Protestants were not the slowest, and therein they were not to be blamed, because the palace of Holyrood House was not thoroughly put in order, for her coming was more sudden than many looked for, she remained in Leith till towards the evening and then repaired thither. In the way between Leith and the Abbey, met her the rebels and crafts of men of whom we spoke of before, to wit, those that had violated the acts of the magistrates and had besieged the provost. But because she was sufficiently instructed that all they did was done in spite of their religion, they were easily pardoned. Fires of joy were set forth at night, and a company of most honest men with instruments of music and with musicians, gave their salutations at her chamber window; the melody, as she alleged, liked her well, and she willed the same to be continued some nights after with great diligence. The Lords repaired to her from all quarters and so was nothing understood but mirth and quietness, till the next Sunday, which was the 24th of August when that preparation began to be made for that idol, the mass to be said in the Chapel, which perceived, the most of all the godly began to speak openly. " Shall that idol be suffered again to take place beneath this realm ? It shall not." The Lord Lindsay (then but master) with the gentlemen of Fife and others plainly cried in the close or yard. " The idolatrous priests shall die the death, according to God's law, One that carried in the candle was evil afraid. But then began flesh and blood to show itself. There durst no Papist neither yet any that came out of France, whisper, but the Lord James, the man whom all the godly did most reverence, took upon him to keep the chapel door. His best excuse was that he would stop all Scottish men to enter into the mass. But it was and is sufficiently known, that the door was kept, that none should have entry to trouble the priest, who after the mass was ended, was committed to the protection of the Lord John of Coldingham and Lord Robert of —— who then were both Protestants and had communicated at the Table of the Lord; betwixt them both the priest was conveyed to the chamber. And so the godly departed with grief of heart, and in the afternoon repaired to the Abbey in great companies. and gave plain signification that they could not abide that the land which God by His power had purged from idolatry, should in their eyes be polluted again and so began complaint. The old duntebors and others that had long served in the court, hoped to have no remission of sins but by virtue of the mass, cried, they would away to France without delay, they could not live without the mass; the same affirmed the Queen's uncle, and would to God, that altogether with the mass, they had taken good night of the realm for ever."

Poor Mary tried to conciliate all parties. She even laid aside the beautiful dress of white crape, by which she had borne the appellation whilst in France of "Reine Blanche;" The White Queen, and put on a sable dress; but this only enhanced her rare beauty, just like the dark background to a glorious picture of celestial penciling. She also issued a proclamation that no alteration should be made in the established religion. On the 2nd of September she made her triumphal entry into Edinburgh. Shortly after and when she finally decided in making Holyrood her abode, she began to give to that ancient Abbey all the luxury and much of the elegance of the French court. She hung all the walls with tapestry, adorned her own person with jewels, and found amusement in landscape gardening, making the old building and all its surroundings appear as if the wand of the magician had been there and not the subtle refined mind of a gentlewoman the young Queen. Among the master spirits of her admirers was Lord James Stuart and though a decided Protestant acted wisely. She created him Earl of Mar which raised the jealousies of the aristocracy, hence trouble ensued, which ended in a war in the north and west. Young Gordon the son of the Earl of Huntly had actually aspired to the Queen's hand, but fighting a duel with Lord Ogilvy he was summoned to Stirling Castle. Instead of obeying the royal mandate, he appeared in open revolt at the head of 1,000 horsemen. His father fortified the castles and awaited the Queen who at the head of a small army went in pursuit of the rebels. Her army was commanded by the Earl of Mar, when they reached the Castle of Inverness, she found the gates shut against her, this made her so determined that she ordered an attack which was successfully carried out, and the captives was put to execution.

No one could display more heroism than the youthful Queen during this short campaign. She endured exposure and wearisome marches, she forded rivers, crossed the highland moors and encamped when necessary amongst the heather, declaring that she regretted "that she was not a man, to know what life it was to lie all night in the fields, or to walk upon the causeway, with a jack and knapsack, a Glasgow buckler and a broadsword." The result of all this was the conquest of the Hamiltons and Gordons, the farther triumph of Protestantism, the augmentation of Murray her brother to greater power; but the prime mover of all, behind the throne, was Knox.

This is how he wrote of the Queen's House. "Three Sunday days, the Queen rode to the Tollbooth, the first day she made a painted oration and there might have been heard among her flatterers "Vox Dianâe, the voice of a goddess! (for it could not be Dei;) and not of woman. God save that sweet face! Was there ever orator spoke so properly and so sweetly, all things—he adds,—misliked the preachers. They spoke boldly against the superfluity of their clothes, and against the rest of their vanity, which they affirmed should provoke God's wrath not only against these foolish women but against the whole realm. Articles were presented for orders to be taken of apparel, and for reformation of other enormities, but all was winked at."

CHAPTER XVIII.

CONTENTS:

Mary's immediate History after her return.—Queen Elizabeth.—Knox.—Marriage of Mary subject of speculation.—Interview between Mary and Knox.

> " I was the Queen of bonnie France
> Where happy I ha'e been,
> Fu' lightly rase I in the morn
> As blythe lay down at e'en."
>
> BURNS.

QUEEN Elizabeth of England was now in all her glory on the English throne. In the winter of 1563 Mary sent a messenger to England regarding the succession. Whilst the embassy was away she gave herself up to all the gaieties of a luxurious court, music, dancing, falconry, poetry and gallantries of every kind passed one after the other in the Palace of Holyrood. In vain the redoubtable Knox and the other ministers mounted their pulpits and thundered anathemas against the court. In one discourse he complained "that princes are more exercised in fiddling and flinging than in reading or hearing of God's most blessed word. Fiddlers and flatterers who commonly corrupt the youth are more precious in their eyes than men of wisdom and gravity, who by wholesome admonition might beat down in them some part of the vanity and pride whereunto all are born but in princes take deep root and strength by wicked education."

The marriage of Mary was a subject of much prophecy and speculation. Knox heard that she had rejected the King of Sweden, but was in more spirit for an Austrian or a Spanish alliance and openly denounced this course of the Queen. Having done so, again he was summoned into the presence of the Queen.

John Erskine of Dun accompanied him into the royal presence. Though the language is ancient spoken at this interview, yet we must give it here as an illustration of Knox's peculiar qualities and Mary's temper. Knox affirms in his record of this interesting interview that the Queen immediately began to weep when he appeared with John Erskine, and exclaimed:

"That never prince was used as she was. I have borne with you in all your rigorous manner of speaking both against myself and against my uncles yea I have sought your favor by all possible means; I offered unto you presence and audience whensoever it pleased you to admonish me; and yet I cannot bequit of you; I vow to God I shall be once revenged," and with these words scarce could Marnocke, one of her pages, get handkerchiefs to hold her eyes dry, for the tears and the howling, besides womanly weeping, stayed her speech."

"The said John did patiently abide all this fume and at opportunity answered. 'True it is, Madame, your Majesty and I have been at diverse controversies into the which I never perceived your Majesty to be offended at me; but when it shall please God to deliver you from that bondage of darknesse and errour wherein ye have been nourished for the lack of true doctrine, your Majesty will find the liberty of my tongue nothing offensive without the preaching place I thinke few have occasion to be offended at me and there I am not master myselfe and must obey Him who commands me to speak plaine, and to flatter no flesh upon the face of the earth."

" But what have you to do," said she, " with my marriage ?"

" If it please your Majesty patiently to hear me I shall show the truth in plain words. I grant your Majesty offered unto me more than ever I required, but my answer was then as it is now, that God hath not sent me to awaite upon the courts of princes or upon the chamber of ladies, but I am sent to preach the Evangell of Jesus Christ to such as please to hear; it hath two points, Repentance and Faith. Now, in preaching repentance, of necessity it is that the sinnes of men are noted, that they may know when they offend. But so it is, that most part of your nobilitie are so much addicted to your affections that neither God's word nor yet their commonwealth, are rightly regarded ; and therefore it becometh me to speak that they may know their duty."

" What have you to do with my marriage, or what are you within the commonwealth ?

" A subject, born within the same, Madame; and albeit I bee neither earle, lord nor baron, within it, yet hath God Madame (how abject that ever I bee in your eyes) a profitable and a usefull member within the same ; yea Madame, to me it appertaineth no less to forewarn of such things as may hurt it, if I foresee them, than it doeth to any one of the nobilitie; for both my vocation and office craveth plainnesse of me; and therefore Madame to yourselfe I say that which I spoke in publike. Whensoever the nobilitie of this realme shall be content and consent, and consent that you be subject to an unlawfnl husband, they doe as much as in them lieth to renounce Christ, to banish the truth, to betray the freedom of this realme, and perchance shall in the end doe small comfort to yourselfe."

"At these words, howling was heard and teares might have been seene in greater abundance than the matter required. John Erskine of Dun, a man of meeke and gentle spirit, stood beside and did what he could to mitigate the anger, and gave unto her many pleasant words of her beauty, of her excellency, and how that all the princes in Enrope would be glad to seek her favors; but all that was to cast oil into the flaming fire."

"No such mitigation, however, was offered by Knox who stood still, without any alteration of countenance, and in the end said; Madam in God's presence I speak, I never delighted in the weeping of any of God's creatures, yea, I can scarcely well abide the teares of mine own boys, when mine own hands correct them; much less, can I rejoice in your Majesties weeping; but seeing I have offered unto you no just occasion if to be offended, but have spoken the truth, as my vocation craves of me; I must sustain your Majesties teares rather than I dare hurt my conscience, or betray the commonwealth by silence."

Herewith was the Queen more offended and commanded the said John to passe forth of the cabinet and to abide further of her pleasure in the Chamber."

"But in that chamber where he stood as one whom men had never seen (except that the Lord Ochiltree bare him company) the confidence of Knox did not provoke him, and, therefore, he began to make discourse with the ladies who were then sitting in all their gorgeous apparel, which, when he espied, he merrily said. " Fair ladies, how pleasant were this life of yours, if it should ever abide, and then in the end that wee might passe to Heaven with geare; but fie upon that knave death, that will come whether we will or not; and when he hath laid on the arrest, then foule wormes will bee busie with this flesh, be it never so faire and so tender and the silly soule, I feare, shall be so feeble, that it can neither carry with it gold, garnishing, targating, pearl nor precious stones."

Knox left the Queen's presence triumphant. At this time Mary had many suitors, some of whom only worshipped at a distance, but one more impetuous than the rest, Captain Hepburn was so familiar and indelicate in his advances that he only escaped punishment by instant flight from Holyrood. Mary's love of gaiety and her dissipation engaged her in many unhappy attentions from emboldend admirers. The side glance when dancing, or the gentle pressure of the hand, these things made the moths flutter round this queenly candle till in the case of more than one, they fell into the flame and were burned to death.

CHAPTER XIX.

CONTENTS:

Murray.—War between Mary and Murray.—Her appearance.—Suitors.—Chastlelard.—Lord Robert Dudley.—Lord Henry Darnley.—Her Marriage with Darnley.—Rizzio.—Lord Ruthven.—Death of Rizzio.—Birth of James VI.—Queen Elizabeth.—Education of the Prince. Quarrels between Mary and Darnley.—Mary makes a tour to the Borders.

> " For ever fortune wilt thou prove
> An unrelenting foe to love,
> And when we meet a mutual heart,
> Come in between and bid us part,
> Bid us sigh on from day to day,
> And wish and wish, the soul away;
> Till youth and genial years are flown
> And all the life of life is gone."
> JAMES THOMSON.

MURRAY, the brother, as he is called of Mary, acts an important part at this period in the History of the Scottish Queen. Siding with the Protestants or Presbyterians and being assured by Queen Elizabeth of her support to the Reformers, the general assembly of the Scottish Kirk was called together by Knox and the Earl of Argyll, and they resolved to petition the Queen to abolish the mass and establish the reformed religion. Murray then headed a plot to surprise Mary and imprison her, which was discovered and the only alternative was general revolt. Murray called the people to arms and Mary summoned her vassals to assemble immediately at Edinburgh, prepared for war. Act-ing on the spur of the moment she actually attended the services of a Presbyterian minister at Callendar to prevent the Reformers from joining Murray, feeling the need of prompt action and having received the Pope's dispensation she created Darnley the Duke of Albany, and marrying him marched forth to meet the enemy. Her force moved so rapidly that Murray was compelled to flee from Stirling to Glasgow and thence to the land of his ally the Earl of Argyll. The fugitive Reformers had now no alternative but to march to Edinburgh. With 1000 men Murray appeared at that metropolis expecting a general uprising in his aid, but the sturdy burghers though hating the religion of the Queen were not prepared to rise in rebellion against her. Mary assembling a force of 1000 men swept Murray's troop as chaff before the wind and compelled him to retreat to the borders of England. Seated on a gallant dashing charger, her perfect form modelled with infinite grace, pistols in her saddlebow and a glow of intense excitement on her lovely face, the Queen indeed looked "every inch a Queen" with a strange fascinating beauty, conquering hearts even amidst the warlike evolutions of her troops.

Leaving Mary and Murray let us return to her other suitors which ended in the marriage of the Queen with Darnley.

Chastelard a poet and musician from the Province of Dauphiny in France, became one of her lovers. He addressed poems to Mary, and she replied to them either by proxy or otherwise, she even allowed private visits of Chastelard in her cabinet and this far more often than to any of her nobility, leading him on by expressions of peculiar regard until he became full of conceit, ambition and passion. Concealing himself one evening under her bed, upon being discovered, the Queen ordered him instantly to leave her presence and the court for ever; not long after the Queen went to Fife and again the same circumstance happened, which so enraged Mary that she ordered Murray to kill him on the spot, but Murray reserved his punishment till two days after when Chastelard was beheaded uttering with his last breath : " Oh ! cruelle dame." The wide spread sensation produced by this execution, tarnished the Queen's reputation and urged upon her the necessity of marrying.

Lord Robert Dudley, son of the Duke of Northumberland was proposed as a suitable match, but another competitor sprung up in the person of Lord Henry Darnley, son of the Earl of Lennox, who had married Lady Margaret Douglas, daughter of Margaret Tudor, widow of James IVth. United thus to both the royal Houses of England and Scotland Darnley was a favorite with the Queen. The young Lord was a shrewd dissembler and a captivating suitor. He placed himself under Murray's guidance, for instance he would go in the morning to hear Knox preach, and in the evening dance a galliard with Mary. Educated a Roman Catholic, he was neither a devotee of Rome nor a strict adherent of Knox.

And now began the struggle between the Reformed religion and the old. Murray who was supported by the Earl of Argyll, Lethington and the

Earl of Leicester in England and Darnley sustained by the Earl of Athol and all the Roman Catholic Barons with Rizzio the Queen's private Secretary.

Murray wished Mary to marry Dudley. She refused and recalled the dissolute Earl of Bothwell from France and commanded Murray to affix his signature to a paper approving of her marriage with Darnley. This he would not do and she charged him with aspiring to the crown. The result was the troublous period mentioned at the beginning of this chapter.

On her receiving the dispensation from the Pope she at once married Darnley, the day previous giving him the title of King. This completely intoxicated the lad's brain for he was only nineteen. On Sunday, Mary and Darnley entered the royal Chapel of Holyrood to be married. The Dean of Restabrig performed the ceremony, not like the gorgeour affair at her former marriage with the Dauphin of France. The Queen kneeled at the altar to hear mass while Darnley retired to hunt. Mary upon reaching her palace put off the sable attire and appeared in a magnificent bridal dress. A grand banquet followed. Darnley had returned from the chase and the Earls of Athol, Morton, Crawford, Eglinton and Carsilles were attendants at the table, whilst Darnley flaunted away in kingly splendour and as a writer justly remarks " Marie Stuart dreamed of a glorious future, as the silence of morning succeeded " music's voluptuous swell," and the hum of excited guests, a brief and delusive vision !"

Having driven Murray into England, Mary under the direction of Rizzio, now began to plot the restoration of the Romish faith. This Rizzio had come to Mary's court in 1562. From the office of a valet he rose to be private Secretary in 1564. Now he was in all the zenith of his ambition. But it could not last. To a man of Darnley's temperament, he soon became an object of distrust. Rizzio was in the pay of the Pope. Like all royal favorites he dressed gorgeously and became haughty and presumptuous. Darnley now became furiously jealous of the Italian and determined to get rid of him by all or any means. This was increased by the Queen's strenuously refusing through Rizzio to bestow on Darnley the crown matrimonial. Brooding over this day by day he at last disclosed his plans to his cousin George Douglas whom he sent to confer with Lord Ruthven. The result of this was that Rizzio would be assassinated and the crown seized.

Lord Ruthven at this time was very ill, but after a short consultation he consented to the plot. It was also made known to Lord Lindsay and Randolph.

Secretly the conspiracy advanced, and no suspicion of evil darkened the days of Rizzio. Mary's friends with those of Lennox had united against Murray and now the adherents of Lennox sought a coalition with Murray to make the blow more successful. Although Queen Elizabeth knew about the intended murder she offered no opposition and Mary was in happy ignorance of it. When the fatal day arrived, which was a Saturday evening, the court yard was suddenly filled with armed men and the shout "A Douglas! a Douglas," reached the ears of the Queen, sitting at tea with some of her courtiers, but before she could ask what it meant, Ruthven in complete armour broke into the room. Mary recoiled at the sight of Ruthven, ghastly white as he was, from lingering disease; but in a moment he said:

"Let it please your Majesty, that yonder man David come forth of your privy chamber where he hath been over long."

The Qneen answered, "What offence hath he done?"

Ruthven replied, "That he made a greater and more heinous offence to her Majesty's honor, the King her husband, the nobility and commonwealth."

"And how?" said she.

"If it would please your Majesty, he hath offended your honor which I dare not be so bold as to speak of, as to the King your husband's honor, he hath hindered him of the crown matrimonial, which your grace promised him, besides many other things which are not necessary to be expressed and hath caused your Majesty to banish a great part of the nobility and to forfeit them, that he might be made a lord. And to your commonwealth he hath been a common destroyer, he drives your Majesty to grant or give nothing but what passes through his hand by taking of bribes of the same; and caused your Majesty to put at the Lord Ross for his whole land, because he would not give over the lands of Meline to the said David, besides many other inconveniences that he solicited your Majesty to do."

"Then her Majesty stood upon her feet and stood before David, he holding her Majesty by the plaits of her gown leaning back over the arch of the window, his dagger drawn in his hand. Meanwhile, Arthur Areskin and the Abbot of Holyrood House, and the Lord Keith master of the Household, with the French apothecary and one of the chamber, tried to lay hands on Lord Ruthven, none of the King's party being then present. Then the said Lord Ruthven pulled out his dagger and defended himself until more came in, and said to them : " Lay no hands on me, for I will not be handled."

" Poor Rizzio cried out in broken language " I am killed." Amid the awful confusion during which the Queen fainted, the terrified secretary was dragged through Mary's bed room into the entrance of her presence chamber, where in spite of Morton's wish to keep him until the next day and hang him, George Douglas, seizing the King's dagger, stabbed him, saying loudly that it was a *Royal Blow*. His comrades rushed on, and did not leave the bleeding form until it was pierced with 56 wounds."

This of course occasioned a great commotion and the Queen pressing the assassins hard, they were obliged to let her know what part her royal husband had taken in the foul and deliberate murder. This murder occasioned the Queen first to spurn Darnley, then to make it up with him, and at last Mary, Darnley and Arthur Erskine her captain of her guard escaped to Dunbar where she issued a proclamation calling on all her loyal subjects to meet her in arms. She then marched to Edinburgh and meanly put the subordinate conspirators to death, whilst the Lords who had been engaged in

Rizzio's murder escaped to England. In justice to themselves these Lords published a manifesto declaring Darnley's complicity in the whole plot which occasioned the first open rupture between them, the Queen lamenting to Melvil Darnley's "folly, ingratitude and misbehavior."

The Queen now left Edinburgh and went to Stirling Castle, where, when she was infant, she had been crowned,—to become a mother. On the 19th of June 1566, a son was born, on whose brow was to sit the diadems of both Scotland and England, James the VIth of Scotland or James Ist of England. The faithful Melvil was immediately sent to Queen Elizabeth with the great news. The Virgin Queen, Good Queen Bess, was in the midst of a magnificent ball, which she had given to her court at Greenwich, when her Secretary of State, Cicil entered the crowded and brilliant room. Towering in all her royal and regal splendour, dressed in magnificent apparel, glittering with gems, the coronet upon her snowy brow and excitement beaming from her flashing eye,—Queen Elizabeth appeared amongst the very many fair and beautiful women of England, A VERY QUEEN. She was dancing at the moment Cicil entered and when he approached, she stopped and he whispered the news into her ear. Like a storm cloud which we see passing for a moment before the shining sun, so a shade for a moment passed over her flushed and kindling features. The magic whirl suddenly ceased and sinking into a chair at hand, she said to the ladies crowding round. "The Queen of Scots is the mother of a fair son, while I am a barren stock." Immediately she regained her self-possession and the brilliant ball proceeded. Next day she sent a messenger to Scotland to congratulate the Queen and assure her of her friendship, though she still gave asylum to the murderers of Rizzio.

Some months passed tranquilly away and the education of the Prince then became a matter of concern. After much trouble it was determined to rear the child in the Reformed faith and thus he as the last King of Scotland as a separate country, was the first of the Scottish Kings who was a Protestant.

Quarrels now became frequent between the Queen and Darnley. At a meeting of council once he rose and addressed the Queen thus " Adieu madame" " you shall not see my face for a long space." Good it would have been both for himself and Mary if he had carried out his determination of leaving the kingdom, but he abandoned it and ultimately fell by his own stupidity. A great gulf now lay between the affection of the Queen and Darnley.

At this time the Queen determined to make a tour of inspection throughout the south-eastern frontier of her kingdom, especially to quell some uprisings of the Johnsons, Armstrongs and Elliots, great chiefs on the borders of England and lying near the lands of the Earl of Bothwell. The Queen was beginning to kindle within her breast a guilty love for this ambitious and misguided man. She had given him a special commission as Lord Lieutenant to repair to the theatre of trouble and endeavor to stop the scenes of bloodshed which were daily being enacted between some of the Border chieftains. According to an old writer, who states, "justice aires were holden annually in the provinces for the administration of justice. Many flagrant enormities having been committed in Liddisdale, it was deemed necessary that the Queen should assist in person in the manner of her predecessors."

CHAPTER XX.

CONTENTS:

The Queen's Border Ride.—Her fever.—Return to Craigmillar Castle.—Hatching Conspiracy.—Christening of James VIth.—Darnley's illness.—Journey to Kirk of Field.—Death of Darnley.

> " Fade, fade, ye flowerets fair,
> Gales fan no more the air,
> Ye streams forget to glide
> Be hushed each vernal strain;
> Since naught can soothe my pain,
> Nor mitigate her pride."
>
> Js. BEATTIE.

THE Earl of Bothwell in the execution of his duties and in a personal combat with John Elliot of Park had received a dangerous wound, and immediately removed to the Castle of Hermitage. The Queen had arrived two days before this at the town of Jedburgh to hold her assizes. Hearing that the Earl was wounded she was as Crawford writes " so highly grieved in heart that she took no repose until she saw him!" Driven by her impatient love, she remained at Jedburgh to the

15th of October she having arrived on the 8th and then conquering all modesty and reserve she took a fleet dashing steed and rode to the Hermitage, attended by Murray and other nobles. She found the Earl pale, faint and languishing, and lavished on him every sentiment of joy consonant to her posision of a wife and mother and Queen. The business of the assizes requiring her immediate presence she left him, and rode back to Jedburgh the whole distance being nearly 40 miles. Arrived at that town she refused to take immediate rest but continued writing to Bothwell till midnight. The result of all this temptation and excitement was that next morning the Queen fell into a swoon and lay for hours at the gates of death. When consciousness returned the beautiful Marie Stuart lay in a burning fever and delirious with the disease. Fearing her last hour when she awoke to sensibility she requested the prayers of the nobles, and confided her son to the care of Elizabeth and sent a messenger to apprise her husband Darnley of her danger.

Thirteen days had passed since that eventful ride when Darnley arrived and finding the Queen much better, he stayed only one night and again set out for Glasgow. This coldness on his part deepened the bitterness of her enmity and at the same time enflamed her devotion for Bothwell. She recovered slowly; journeying liesurely with careful conveyance and frequent rest the Queen arrived at Craigmillar Castle three miles from Edinburgh where she took rooms. Here was hatched and at last carried into execution one of the most deliberate murders in the annals of crime. DeCroc writing to the Archbishop of Glasgow, says: "The Queen is not well. I do believe the principal part of her disease to consist of a deep grief and sorrow. Nor does it seem possible to make her forget the same. Still she repeats the words, "I could wish to be dead." Lethington also a shrewd observer writes: "It is an heart-break for her to think that she should see her husband, and how to be free of him she sees no outlet."

This caused several of her nobles to unite for the relief of the Queen. This same Lethington arranged a plan daring in the extreme and full of hazard and danger. He proposed the return of the murderers of Rizzio with a free pardon, the divorce of Darnley and if need be his assassination. The Earl of Bothwell already seeing the ultimatum of all his hopes within his grasp, eagerly joined the plot. The Earls of Argyll and Huntly assented. Even Murray was anxious that his sister should have a divorce from Darnley. When the scheme was broached to the Queen she answered "that on two conditions she might agree to the proposal." The first that the divorce should be made lawfully, second it should not prejudice her son, otherwise she should rather endure all torments and abide the perils that might ensue.

After further parley, Lethington closed the conference by saying: "Madam, let us guide the business among us and your grace shall see nothing but good, and approved by Parliament."

Immediately after this interview an act of Parliament was hurried through and passed in which the Lords entered into a bond and solemn oath " to cut off the King as a young fool and tyrant, who was an enemy to the nobility, and had conducted himself in an intolerable manner to the Queen." Pledging themselves to be faithful the bond was signed by Sir James Balfour, Huntly, Lethington and Argyll and given into the keeping of Bothwell.

A few weeks later at Stirling Castle amid pomp and show James VIth was christened. Bothwell was master of ceremonies, Darnley was not present at all. Queen Elizabeth had appointed the Countess of Argyll to represent her as godmother and had sent a golden font worth $5,000 to be used at the ceremony. The infant was called Charles James. Shortly after the christening of James, his mother pardoned and restored Morton, Ruthven Lindsay and seventy-six more of the murderers and conspirators of Rizzio's death. This greatly alarmed Darnley who quitted Stirling and went to Glasgow to his father's house. The small pox was then very prevalent and Darnley caught the loathesome disease which prostrated him to the verge of the grave. Whilst recovering from his sickness Mary left Edinburgh for Glasgow. There on the arrival of the Queen a kind of compromise and reconciliation took place. Mary at length says one of her biographers " with her gentle persuasion, tearful and lustrous blue eyes, subdued reproaches and expressions of affection, won the confidence of the vacillating, miserable phantom of royalty."

Darnley begged the Queen to leave him no more. She wished him then to go to Craigmillar Castle. He consented, if she would receive him to her heart as her true husband. To this she assented, gave him her hand as a pledge but told him to keep the reconciliation a secret for fear of the Lords, and all would be well. Her biographer again writes here, " The mind pauses over this scene, bewildered and sad. To believe Mary entirely sincere in so great and sudden a transition of manner, is an amplitude of charitable credulity it would be pleasant to award. To doubt her truthfulness is to people the obscurity of a woman's heart, with more demoniac inmates, than the deepest depravity in time would seem to warrant. By whatever reasons enforced by a false training, she hushed the upbraidings of conscience, the conclusion of perfidy is inevitable."

At last Darnley set out on that journey which ended in " that bourne from which no traveller returns." Arrived at Edinburgh, the conspirators sent him to the Kirk of Field. But the mind of Darnley was distressed with the apprehension of treachery. He said to Crawford. " I have fears enough, but may God judge between us, I have her promise only to trust to, but I have put myself into her hands and shall go with her, though she should murder me." Bothwell met the Queen and Darnley not far from Edinburgh and on the 31st January, Darnley entered the House of Kirk of Field from which he never went alive.

On Sabbath evening the Queen came to his room and conversed familiarly with him, then, when all was ready, she recollected that she had promised to be present at a merry making in the palace on the occasion of the marriage of one of her servants. She then tenderly kissed the fevered lips of Darnley and taking a loving farewell left, hastening with her suite and Bothwell to the festival. By a very remarkable coincidence, the proper Psalms for the English Evening Service of the day contained these words. " My heart is disquieted within me, and the fear of death is fallen upon me. Fearfulness and trembling are come upon me, and an horrible dread hath overwhelmed me. And I said oh that I had wings like a dove for then would I flee away and be at rest."

Trembling at these startling and prophetic words which he had read before going to bed and after the excitement of fear had partially subsided, the poor desolate young King fell asleep, soon to be " that sleep which knows no waking."

About midnight the assassins entered the chamber and strangling the page seized the weak King who soon was gasping for life in their grasp, then shortly after a terrific explosion was heard and Kirk of Field was blown into a thousand fragments.

The body of Darnley, though many of the bystanders saw that it had no " smell of fire on the garments," was ordered by Bothwell to be taken away and it was privately buried in the Chapel of Holyrood.

Mary pretended much sorrow, but it took the form of silent dejection. She displayed none of the laudable energy with which she hunted the murderers of Rizzio. She would see none but Bothwell. The poor menials as in Rizzio's case were consigned to the hands of the executioner, but by their testimony and that of others, the circumstantial evidence of Mary's guilt from Glasgow to the fatal evening is so conclusive that we are bound to say she was the guilty person, who only employed subordinates to execute her purposes. And again quoting the author already mentioned, we may say: "This conviction of her guilt at the tribunal of unbiased judgment, however reluctantly allowed, is only a simple item of proof, darkening the historic annals of a fallen race, that intellect, beauty, and pride of place are no security against the insidious and destructive power of unsubdued selfishness taking the descending channel of wild and stormy passion. Nothing but Christian humility and trust in an Infinite Guide, can save, amid strong temptations, immorality, in a hovel or on a throne, from the strand of moral ruin."

CHAPTER XXI.

CONTENTS:

Movements of the Queen after the death of Darnley.—Popular Feeling.—Elizabeth's Letter.—Intimacy with Bothwell. — Mock trial of Bothwell. — Acquittal. — Mary's devotion to Bothwell.—Her return to Edinburgh.—Seduction of Mary by Bothwell.—Marriage of Mary and Bothwell.

"Vaulting ambition."
SHAKESPEARE.

WRITING to the Archbishop of Glasgow immediately after the commission of the terrible tragedy Mary pretended that she by a fortunate chance was saved from sharing the fate of Darnley and pretends all ignorance of the horrid deed. Although ominous placards and other means were tried to warn the Queen, yet she was intoxicated with guilty love towards Bothwell, and when she went to Seton to lull popular excitement, he followed her thither, and though all the country were mourning for the poor young King; Mary and he would shoot at the butts against Huntly and Seton, whilst the court at Seton was occupied in gay amusements. But at Edinburgh the people were not so easily put down or cowered. When they openly denounced both the Queen and Bothwell, the latter rode with fifty horsemen into Edinburgh and publicly said that he knew who were the authors of the placards and he would "wash his hands in their blood," but this availed nothing.

Elizabeth sent a letter to Mary in which she declared that she was astonished and terrified at what she had heard. The latter part of her letter ran thus: "Think of me I beg you who would not entertain such a thought in my heart for all the gold in the world, I exhort you, I advise and beseech you to take this thing so much at heart, as not to fear to bring to judgment the nearest relation you have and to let no persuasion hinder you from manifesting to the world that you are a noble princess and also a loyal wife."

Even in France the impression spread that Mary was guilty but she continued week after week to do nothing to vindicate her sullied honor. The infatuated Queen was unmoved in her fidelity towards Bothwell who now began to behave as all other royal favorites have done, in an imperious, insolent manner.

His mock trial was a farce and the indefinite indictment against him, being read in court, whilst Lennox not being allowed to appear against him he was of course acquitted. When Mary appointed him to the high position of high admiral, Lennox fled to England and Murray to France. When nothing would stop the Queen in her infatuated career Lord Herries fearlessly told her not to marry the man whom all the country believed to be the real murderer of the King but failing in his mission he had barely time to escape from the hands of Bothwell. At last the Earl invited to a banquet the Earls of Morton, Argyll, Huntly, Sutherland, Eglinton and many other Lords and openly told them he intended to marry Mary and asked their consent. Cowed by the presence of armed men this consent was given.

In the meantime Bothwell began to exhibit his unrestrained temper in uncivil deportment even towards the Queen. He wished to hurry on the wedding but the time was too short after the death of Darnley, so they resorted to a ruse, which was nothing more or less than that Bothwell should meet the Queen on her return from Stirling Castle, whither she had gone to visit her young son and carry her off. On the 21st April 1567 Mary Stuart proceeded to Stirling Castle. On the 24th she left it and had proceeded as far as Almond Bridge when she was met by Bothwell and six hundred horsemen. He seized Mary's horse and led her without conflict to his own Castle of Dunbar. This was the first act in that guilty drama, the next was to divorce his beautiful wife Lady Jane Gordon. This was soon accomplished and the same day that the divorce arrived from St. Andrews, the Queen returned to Edinburgh. When she came to the gate of the city, the Earl with great respect laid his hand on the bridle of Mary's horse, and his soldiers then threw down their spears as the signal that their Sovereign was not only free, but that their Lord and master was no more than an humble unprotected servant of Her Majesty.

Immediately after this the Banns of Marriage between Mary and Bothwell were publicly declared and when the Queen made him Duke of Orkney and Shetland and with her own hand gave him the coronet his pride was full. Two days after this she signed the marriage contract and the next morning the nuptials were celebrated in Holyrood palace according to the Roman Catholic ceremony, and in the Protestant Church by the Bishop of Orkney. Small indeed was the attendance of the nobility but there was in the event, instead of joy as should have been in a royal marriage, long heralding future good to the popular mind, something which they felt was the forerunner of great national future calamity. The tidings spread early next morning that the Queen had married Bothwell and on the gate of the Palace of Holyrood was found attached a celebrated line from the poet Ovid.

" Mense malas maio nubere ait."

Strange it need not seem that such a disgusting marriage three months after the foul murder of Darnley, was not a day old, before there was a domestic quarrel, but such was the case. De Croc wrote to Charles IX of France and to Catherine "that it is a very unfortunate one and already is repented of." Yesterday being in the closet with the Earl of Bothwell, she called out aloud for some one to give her a knife that she might kill herself. Those who were in the adjoining room heard her. They think that unless God aid her, she will fall into despair."

CHAPTER XXII.

CONTENTS:

Confederacy of Nobles.—The Queen goes to Borthwick Castle.— "Borthwick Castle." — "The House of Borthwick".—Origin and History of the Name and House.— Carberry Hill.—Its results.—Fate of Bothwell.—Return to Edinburgh.—Lochleven Castle.—Escape of Mary.—Battle of Langside.—Queen Mary's Watch.—Her flight to England.—James VI.

> "Had we never loved sae kindly,
> Had we never loved sae blindly,
> Never met or never parted,
> We had ne'er been broken hearted."
>
> BURNS.

MARY now despatched ambassadors to the foreign courts to obtain their recognition of Bothwell as her husband. She pretended that the nobility had urged her marriage with him, but all this was of no avail for the same confederacy of nobles which had formerly taken arms against Bothwell now bound themselves together in solemn covenant to free themselves and their Prince from the assumptions and pride of such an usurper. At last the slumbering rebellion broke out. " The names of the Lords that convened in Stirling were the Earls of Argyll, Morton, Athol and Mar. There is to be joined with the four forenamed lords the Earls of Glencairn, Cassillis, Montrose, Caithness, the Lords Boyd, Ochiltree, Ruthven, Drummond, Gray, Glamnis, Innermeith, Lindsay, Hume and Herries."

Though the forces of the nobility increased daily, infatuated Mary was fearless, and ignorant of their movements and numbers, as well as of impending danger. In the midst of all this commotion Bothwell demanded the keeping of the young Prince. His guardian the Earl of Mar refused, unless young Prince James were placed in the Castle of Edinburgh and under the care of an honorable and unimpeachable governor.

The Queen to escape the troubles surrounding her and the harassed atmosphere of her own follies had left Edinburgh and at this time was quietly enjoying herself in BORTHWICK CASTLE a fine structure which had been built by LORD BORTHWICK, A. D. 1430. The present Lord, *William, Sixth Lord Borthwick* was a steady friend and supporter of Mary, as his father *John, Fifth Lord Borthwick* had been a firm supporter of her mother, Mary of Guise, against " The Lords of the Congregation."

It may seem presumptuous in allotting a whole section of a chapter to the History of the House of Borthwick, but from the earliest ages of Scottish History, the members of this house have played an important part therein. As has been already stated, the first of this name in Scotland is said to have been ANDREAS the son of the LORD OF BURTICK in Livonia who accompanied Edgar Atheling and his two sisters Margaret and Christina to Scotland in 1067. The elder sister Margaret as we have seen became wife of Malcom Canmore and Queen of Scotland and after her death was canonized by the name of St. Margaret. Andreas Borthwick obtained from the King some lands in the county of Selkirk and these lands with the stream running through them he called BORTHWICK from his name which appellation they continue to have to this day.

In the reign of David II, the House of Borthwick is mentioned regarding the patrimony of Borthwick and in the reign of Robert II, Sir William Borthwick was possessed of the lands of Catkume in Edinburghshire 1378.

During the fifteenth and following centuries the Lords of Borthwick had immense possessions and great influence in that portion of Mid-Lothian which now forms the parish of Borthwick and surrounding districts, a locality which has ever been famed for its romantic scenery.

The first Lord Borthwick was Sir William Borthwick of Borthwick, in the reign of James I of Scotland. He was the son of Sir William Borthwick, Senr. whose two daughters married (the eldest,) James Douglas, Lord Dalkeith and afterwards George Crichton, Earl of Caithness, and (the youngest) Sir John Oliphant.

This first Lord as has already been said built "BORTHWICK CASTLE." He was the cupbearer to

St. Clair, Earl and Prince of Orkney, who maintained his court at Roslin Castle, with regal magnificence. He and his lady were buried in Borthwick Church. They left two sons the elder becoming William IInd Lord Borthwick the second John de Borthwick acquired the lands of Crookston and his descendants now possess the property in which the ruins of Borthwick Castle stand, having purchased them.

The 2nd Lord left three sons, the eldest becoming the 3rd Lord and the other two, were Sir Thomas and Sir James. This Lord was slain at the Battle of Flodden, leaving two sons, William his successor and Alexander Borthwick of Nenthorn.

The fourth Lord was appointed tutor of the King and commander of Stirling Castle. After this he died A. D. 1542. His eldest son had died before him and the only other son became John, 5th Lord Borthwick.

The fifth Lord opposed the Reformation steadily and declared "that he would believe as his fathers had done before him." He greatly assisted the Queen Regent against the Lords of the Congregation. Dying in A. D. 1565 he left one son William, 6th Lord Borthwick. This Lord was a great and steady friend of Queen Mary. Frequently the Queen visited the Castle of Borthwick and at last escaped there with Bothwell, whence she left two days after her arrival in man's apparel. This Lord left two sons William who died before his father and James, the 7th Lord. Very little is recorded of this Lord. He was succeeded by his son John, eighth Lord Borthwick, who dying was succeeded by his only son John, the ninth Lord. This Lord adhered firmly to the royal cause during all the time of the civil war. After the Battle of Dunbar, Borthwick Castle, heroically held out till artillery was brought to bear upon it. As no relief came he surrendered on honorable terms and was allowed liberty to march out with his wife (Lady Elizabeth Ker, second daughter of William, third Earl of Lothian) and all the household and retainers. He died A. D. 1672 without issue and the title became dormant till the year 1727. After some delay Henry Borthwick male heir of Alexander Borthwick of Nenthorn succeeded by decision of the House of Lords A. D. 1762 as 10th Lord Borthwick. In A. D. 1772 he died, without issue and the title again became dormant.

Various competitors afterwards sprung up for the title, Archibald Borthwick the 10th Lord's heir male was in Norway at the time of his death. In 1807 his claim was resisted by John Borthwick of Crookston and David Borthwick grand-father of the Author of these sketches, the one claiming direct descent from the 1st Lord Borthwick through nine generations, the other claiming from the 2nd son of the 2nd Lord. These disputes continued year after year till at last A. D. 1870. Cunningham Borthwick; 2nd only surviving son of Patrick Borthwick who was the son of Archibald Borthwick before mentioned as being in Norway succeeded to the title as 11th Lord Borthwick. This Lord was born A. D. 1813 at Edinburgh and married A. D. 1865, Alice Harriet daughter of Thomas H. Day, Esq. and has only one son, the present heir to the ancient House of Borthwick. Thus, there are now only two lives between the title and the eldest brother of these sketches, Revd. Hugh Jamieson Borthwick of Pembina, Manitoba, Canada.

Leaving the Queen at Borthwick Castle, Bothwell proceeded to Melrose to arrange an expedition against Lord Home and then returned to Borthwick. On the 11th June the confederacy of the Lords appeared before that strong fortress. Bothwell having timely warning of their approach, privately escaped to Dunbar, where Queen Mary dressed as a page followed him two days after. One short month from their unhappy marriage day the two armies confronted each other on Carberry Hill on the very same ground which the English had held at the disastrous battle of Pinkie. The Queen's forces consisted of 4000 men of the Lothians and Merse. They were commanded by Bothwell in person, having under him Lords Seton, Yester and Borthwick with four powerful Barons of the Merse, viz: Wedderburn, Langton, Crunledge and Hirsel, also those of the Bass, Waughton, Ormiston of Lothian and Ormiston of that Ilk in Tiviotdale. The confederate army was led by Lord Home and the Earl of Morton who was afterwards Regent. Bothwell mounted on a splendid steed offered by single combat to decide the quarrel. Eagerly did Kirkaldy of Grange accept the proffered gage, but Bothwell declared he would not fight with an inferior. He afterwards challenged Morton himself, who instantly accepted and it was ordered to be fought on foot; then old Lord Lindsay of the Byres requested the general to allow him to meet Bothwell as the next of kin to the murdered Darnley. Just as the twenty selected knights on each side had arranged every thing, the Queen by her royal prerogative forbade the combat and demanded a conference. Kirkcaldy approached and meekly kneeling before the Queen requested her to quit the traitor Bothwell and join herself with her true lords who only wanted her safety and happiness. Bothwell ordered one of his harquebussiers to shoot him and whilst the man was in the act of doing so the Queen saw him and uttering a scream, threw herself before the levelled piece and cried to Bothwell that surely he would not disgrace her so far as to murder one to whom she had promised protection.

Bothwell then took leave of the Queen and rode off the field with a few followers. For some days he lurked about Dunbar and afterwards fled to the north, then to Norway and after that the poor miserable outcast died a maniac in a Danish dungeon, April 1578.

> " A fugitive among his own,
> Disguised, deserted. desolate,
> A weed upon the torrent thrown,
> A Cain among the sons of men,
> A pirate on the ocean then,
> A Scandinavian captive's doom,
> To die amid the dungeon's gloom."
>
> DELTA.

" Thus perished, says Kirkaldy, the chief of the Hepburns, whose sounding titles of " the most potent and noble Prince James Duke of Orkney,

Marquis of Fife, Earl of Bothwell, Lord of Hales, of Crichton, Liddisdale and Zetland; High admiral of Scotland; Warden of the three Marches; High Sheriff of Edinburgh, Haddington and Berwick; Baillie of Lauderdale, Governor of Edinburgh Castle and Captain of Dunbar"—only served to make the scene of the fettered felon, expiring in the dungeons of Draxholm, a more striking example of retributive fate, and of that guilty ambition, misdirected talent and insatiable pride, the effect of which had filled all Europe with horror and amazement."

The Queen then approached the Lord of Grange and extending her delicate hand which he kissed she said that she submitted to his guidance; he then took the bridle of her horse and conducted her into the middle of the confederate army. They reverently received the Queen who with a clear voice said: " My Lords I am come to you, not out of any fear I had of my life nor yet doubting of the victory, if matters had gone to the worst but I abhor the shedding of Christian blood, especially of those that are my own subjects and therefore I yield to you, and will be ruled hereafter by your counsels, trusting you will respect me as your born Princess and Queen."

Then began the march to Edinburgh, which when they had reached they placed the Queen in the Provost's house and next day after consultation determined to send her a prisoner to Lochleven Castle which was immediately done. On the 11th June Mary "mounted on a sorry hackney" attired in coarse cassock and guarded by the savage Ruthven and Lindsay entered the Castle. This Castle now in ruins, was owned by William Douglas, the half brother of Murray and Margaret Erskine his mother was the Queen's mortal enemy. Soon after, the Lords compelled her to sign her abdication and place Murray as Regent which she did with eyes suffused with tears and a trumulous hand. Immediately the nobles gathered at Stirling and crowned the young prince by the title of James VIth. He was only thirteen months old at the time and the great Reformer preached the sermon on the august occasion. Mary herself when an infant had also been crowned in this old renowned fort. In the mean time Murray returned from France and immediately visited the Queen at Lochleven and then repaired to Stirling and afterwards to the Tolbooth in Edinburgh when he was sworn in as Regent. He also gave orders that his sister should be more leniently treated. Margaret Erskine's youngest son George Douglas became smitten with Mary's surpassing beauty. The magic which fell upon all hearts from her deep lovely eye and the wondrous fascination of her graceful person made the young man a creature of her will. He resolved to obtain her liberty and her hand. Disguising the Queen in the apparel of a laundress who frequented the Castle he led her unsuspected to the margin of the lake. The boat glided away from the shore and Mary's heart beat fast as she thought of her regaining her liberty, but one of the boatmen wanting to lift her veil, she pnt up her white purely shaped hand and betrayed herself. Nothing remained but to row back to the Castle and deliver the fair captive into the Laird of Lochleven's hands.

In the meanwhile George Douglas, her lover was not idle. He resolved on another plan. It was this. At the hour of meals the doors of the fortress were all shut and the keys laid beside the castellan or governor. When the appointed time arrived, the page also of the name of Douglas placed the plate before the Laird, and dropping the napkin over the keys, bore them unobserved away. He hastened to Mary, who attired in a servant's dress followed him through the gate and they then locked the doors and threw the keys into the lake. These keys were found not many years ago by a person fishing near the ruins of Lochleven Castle. The Queen and Douglas then stepped into the boat that was waiting and quickly rowed across the lake. Just as soon as she reached the shore, Lord Seton and others joined her and mounting a splendid charger standing ready for her, she and her Lords dashed away at full gallop towards Niddry Castle the seat of Lord Seton. Resting a few hours there, she again rode at full speed to the strong fortress of Hamilton where she was met by Lord Claud Hamilton and fifty horsemen.

The tidings of her deliverance flew like wild fire or the morning light, throughout the length and breadth of Bonnie Scotland, and the friends of her former days who had ever continued loyal to the Stuart throne, and all the forgiven Lords and the disaffected ones towards Murray thronged around her to offer once more their love and their lives to the beautiful Marie the Queen of Scotland. No less than forty bishops, earls and lords and a hundred barons signed a league to place the crown once more on her beauteous brow. In the presence of her council she revoked her abdication, declared Murray to be a traitor and found herself in the briefest space of time at the head of a force of 6000 men all determined to die in her cause.

In the meantime Murray was not idle, calmly he acted when he heard the news. His well arranged plans inspired his partizans with courage and drew to his standard all the Presbyterian soldiery. Edinburgh instantly gave him 400 of her best hackbutters. Glasgow offered her strength and Dunbar Castle repelled Mary's demand for surrender. The Earl of Mar hurried to the camp the trained men and all the heavy ordnance of Stirling Castle; from the Merse country brave Alexander Hume brought up his 600 lancers. Morton, Glencairn and the venerable Laird of Grange brought forth their recruits from every valley and down every hill side, till round them stood a solid phalanx of 3000 strong and fearless men. Those, with all the others gave Murray a well disciplined army of between four and five thousand men. The contending armies met at Langside. The heights of Langside were occupied by the Laird of Grange, who placed a company of hackbutters in ambush and near a lane through which the Queen's troops had to march to reach the hill. This path led through a narrow defile intersected with hedges and guarded by plantations, with dwellings dotted all through them. The Queen's cavalry though vastly superior in numbers to that of Murray's found it impossible to fight there in the narrow pathway. The followers of Hamilton 2000 strong entered the defile with the firm step of warriors marching on to victory and with the wings of conquest enfolding their standard when suddenly like the lightning's flash or a storm of hail from a viewless cloud in the blue empyrean of upper ether, a devastating wasting fire was poured upon them from the ambuscade and upon the astonished and panic stricken vanguard. Confusion worse confounded took possession of the ranks, the living pressing up the declivity and being mowed down by the terrible discharges of the unseen foe. When they by superhuman exertions reached the summit to their horror again they were met by the enemy and this time by Murray and his valorous pikemen who rushed like giants to the desperate conflict. The heroic Laird of Grange swept on from one avenging aim to another, to reanimate and reinforce his mountain warriors. Brave Morton with the precision of a geometical problem manœuvred his troops and cut down all that came in his victorious career; —Hume dashed like a wild impetuous torrent from the Grampian Hills and utterly broke the ranks of the enemy, whilst Murray himself made a brilliant and decisive charge with his resistless soldiers on the reeling disappearing ranks of his sister and the terrible flow of brothers' blood was over and the victory won. So complete was the triumph that in less than one hour from the commencement of the engagement the hapless Queen had 300 left dead on that bloody eminence, resounding lately from the shouts and noise of "battles magnificent array" but now with the air filled by the moans and groans of scores of poor wretches crying for water and help in their bitter agony. From the top of an eminence the

Queen had observed the arena of battle and now seeing all was over, she descended with haste to the plain and mounting a horse attended by a few faithful servants and friends. She neither halted nor stopped nor slackened her speed till she had placed no less a distance than 60 miles between herself and her now inveterate foes. Faint and weary the cavalcade arrived at a lonely cottar's and asked for food. The guidewife had nothing but oat cake and milk to set before her guests. Queen Mary ate greedily of the simple fare and when about to leave for Dundrennan Abbey, she gave as a parting gift to the hind or cottar, her beautiful gold watch and a remarkably fine solitaire, saying that their fugitive Queen needed them no more. These antiques remained in the possession of the Torrance family till last year, when at the death of the Revd Alexander Torrance, Presbyterian and Parish Minister of Glencross, near Edinburgh, they were willed by him to the Antiquarian Society of that city. Large sums had been offered to the Revd. gentleman during his life time for Queen Mary's watch but they were invariably refused, as it was an heir loom and had descended from father to son through many generations.

When the Queen arrived at Dundrennan Abbey she gazed a moment on the waters, and shortly after chose a vessel in which she embarked for England instead of France.

Queen Elizabeth having heard of her arrival on English soil gave the royal fugitive a royal journey from Workington to Carlisle. After some little time, war ceased in Scotland and the Regent made preparations to confront his sister. At this time the Duke of Norfolk secretly aspired to the hand of Mary Stuart;—but his designs were discovered by Elizabeth, and this made Mary be more closely confined and the Duke arrested. He was shortly after tried of aspiring to the throne, and sentenced to death, which he endured with unflinching calmness.

At this time the Regent Murray was basely shot by a fanatic of the opposite side. Whilst passing through the town of Linlithgow, James Hamilton his mortal enemy assassinated him, and escaped. He was succeeded by the Earl of Lennox who shortly after was shot in the scuffle (1571) between the Earl of Huntly and the garrison of Stirling. He was succeeded by Mar and the whole country was divided between the King's men and the Queen's men, that is those who followed the Regent and the Lords of the Congregation with their youthful King and those who still adhered to the unfortunate Queen. Mar died and was succeeded by Morton who soon fell by the hands of a confederacy into disgrace and was beheaded by "The Maiden" a kind of guillotine still to be seen in the Museum of the Antiquarian Society of Edinburgh.

No one succeeded Morton and the young King nominally governed the kingdom. In the mean time his mother continued being sent from fortress to fortress, from castle to castle, till at last she was ordered by the English Queen to be kept a prisoner in Fotheringay Castle. Here she lived a lonely prisoner, and from the time she entered England to her execution was no less than the long period of nineteen years.

CHAPTER XXIV.

CONTENTS:

Mary's captivity.— Poetry.—Burns' Queen Mary.—Poetry.—Execution.—Spanish Armada.—Macauly's poem on the Armada.

I

" There's none to soothe my soul to rest
   There's none my load of grief to share,
Or wake to joy this lonely breast,
   Or light the gloom of dark despair.
Oft to the winds my grief I tell,
   They bear along the mournful tale,
To dreary echo's rocky cell,
   That heaves it back upon the gale.

II

The little wild birds merry lay,
   That wont my lightsome heart to cheer,
In murmuring echoes dies away,
   And melts like sorrow on my ear,
The voice of love no more can cheer
   The look of love no more can warm,
Since mute for aye's that voice so dear,
   And closed that eye alone could charm.

JAMES YOOL.

DURING her captivity in the various forts and castles to which she had been remanded, Queen Mary ever found a little rest and repose in the com position of poetry in the French language of which she was passionately fond and in her voluminous letters written to various personages during her sad period of incarceration. We have only space to insert one of her poetical pieces which was written it is presumed at Tutbury where she had been confined for some years previous to her being sent to Fotheringay Castle.

> "Que suis-je, hélas! et de quoy sert ma vie?
> Je ne suis fors qu'un corps privé de cueur,
> Un ombre vain, un objet de malheur,
> Qui n'a plus rien que de mourir envie,
> Plus ne portez, ô ennemis, d'amie,
> A qui n'a plus l'esprit à la grandeur!
> La consommé d'excessive doulleur;
> Votre ire en brief se voirra assouvie,
> Et vous, amys, qui m'avez tenu chère
> Souvenez-vous que sans heur, sans santay,
> Je ne scaurois auqun bonne œuvre fayre,
> Souhatez donc fin de calamitay;
> Et que sa bas estant assez puné
> J'aie ma part en la joie infinie."

To this must be added Robert Burns' beautiful lament of Queen Mary, where she says:

> "Now Nature hangs her mantle green
>   On lika blooming tree,
> And spreads her sheets o' daisies white
>   Out ower the grassy lea.
>
> Now Phœbus cheers the crystal streams,
>   And glads the azure skies,

But nocht can glad the weary wicht,
   That fast in durance lies.

Now blooms the lily by the bank,
   The primrose doun the brae;
The hawthorn's budding in the glen,
   And milk-white is the slae.

Now laverocks wake the merry morn,
   Aloft on dewy wing,
The merle, in his noontide bower,
   Makes woodland echoes ring.

The mavis, mild wi' mony a note,
   Sings drowsy day to rest;
In love and freedom they rejoice,
   Wi' care nor thrall opprest.

The meanest hind in fair Scotland
   May rove these sweets amang;
But I, the queen o' a' Scotland,
   Maun lie in prison strang.

I was the queen o' bonnie France,
   Where happy I ha'e been;
Fu' lightly rase I in the morn,
   As blythe lay down at e'en.

And I'm the sovereign of Scotland,
   And mony a traitor there;
Yet here I lie in foreign band,
   And never-ending care.

But as for thee, thou false woman
   My sister and my fae,

Grim vengeance yet shall whet a sword,
   That through thy soul shall gae.

The weeping blood in woman's breast,
   Was never known to thee,
Nor the balm that draps on wounds of wae,
   From woman's pitying e'e.

My son ! my son ! may kinder stars
   Upon thy fortune shine,
And may those pleasures gild thy reign,
   That ne'er would blink on mine.

God keep thee frae thy mother's faes,
   Or turn their hearts to thee ;
And where thou meet'st thy mother's friend,
   Remember him for me.

Oh, soon to me may summer sun
   Nae mair licht up the morn !
Nae mair, to me, the autumn winds
   Wave o'er the yellow corn.

And in the narrow house o' death
   Let winter round me rave,
And the next flowers that deck the spring
   Bloom on my peaceful grave !

And now drew near the saddest period of the life of this eventful Queen. On account of the conspiracy of Babington and others the royal commission went forth that Mary should be executed. The sonnet below, with the near close of her existence in view, is a sad melancholy evidence of poetical genius which through years of suffering, had seldom breathed the moan of the captive even in poetic verse, was written in a legible hand on a large sheet of paper and translated into English reads thus:

> "Alas! what am I and in what estate,
> A wretched case, bereaved of its heart,
> An empty shadow, lost, unfortunate;
> To die is now in life my only part,
> Foes to my greatness let your envy rest;
> In me no taste for grandeur now is found,
> Consumed by grief, with heavy ills opprest,
> Your wishes and desires will soon be crowned,
> And you, my friends, who still have held me dear
> Be think you, that when health and heart are fled
> And every hope of future good is dead.
> 'Tis time to wish our sorrows ended here,
> And that this punishment on earth is given,
> That I may live to endless bliss in Heaven."

The history of the last month of Queen Mary's life in prison has been written by many authors but chief among them all in exactness of details, in faithful portrayal of her character and in the individuality of all that figured in the sad events is the German poet Schiller who incorporated these melancholy days into his play of "*Mary Stuart.*" Let us give the following word picturing of one of the saddest scenes of her career, taken from his plays.

The scene is laid in the second story stone corridor of Fotheringay prison. The Queen has been summoned to descend the stairs to the floor below, where the fatal axe and block are waiting. She is the central figure of the group, who have been awaiting her appearance. She is sumptuously arrayed in a royal purple velvet dress, a rosary hangs from her girdle, and from it a crucifix depends. A diadem of precious stones binds her hair; her large black veil is thrown back, and she is addressing her old and valued friend and house-steward, Sir Andrew Melvil, who has just arrived after an absence of many months, and has been graciously permitted to converse with her. As she approaches, the venerable counselor throws himself upon his knees before her and pays obeisance to his only recognized sovereign. She addresses him in these words:

"How! Melvil here! My worthy sir, not so;
Arise; you rather come in time to see
The triumph of your mistress, than her death.
One comfort which I never yet expected
Is granted me: that, after death, my name
Will not be quite abandoned to my foes;
One friend at least, one partner of my faith
Will be my witness in the hour of death.
Say, honest Melvil, how you far'd the while.
*   *   *   *   *   *
Sir, to your loyal bosom I commit
My latest wishes. Bear then, sir, my blessing
To the most Christian king, my brother,
And the whole royal family of France;
I bless the Cardinal, my honored uncle,
And also Henry Guise, my noble cousin.
I bless the Holy Father, the Viceregent
Of Christ on earth, who will, I trust, bless me.

I bless the King of Spain, who nobly offered
Himself as my deliv'rer, my avenger—
They are all remembered in my will. I hope
That they will not despise, how poor so e'er
They be, the presents of a heart which loves thee."

The Queen then extends her left hand above the old man's head as she blesses him, while her right hand, in which she holds the handkerchief which she subsequently presented to Margaret Curl, is grasped by the right hand of her nurse and attendant, Hannah Kennedy, who stands at her side tendering the support which may be needed by the Queen. There is no despair nor shrinking from her fate, no frenzy nor passionate outcry. She is calm, prepared, resolute, and queenly.

As Melvil hears her appeal he lifts up his bald head fringed with white hair, and with outstretched arms exclaims, in the language of the play, Act V., Scene VI.:

"I swear obedience in the name of all."

The most intense devotion, coupled with sorrow and grief, is his. He has served his Queen and mistress faithfully through her life. He will not desert her at its close, nor let her name be reproached after she has gone.

At the left hand side of the Queen, and a little behind, are grouped the three ladies of her chamber—Alice, Gertrude, and Rosamund—whom she next addresses, leaving them her pearls and garments. The first of these, who stands in the centre and a trifle in advance of her two fellows, has her hands clasped and her eyes upturned in devout prayer for her mistress, while a look of the most intense suffering is upon her mobile face. Gertrude has her face buried in her handkerchief, and is weeping bitterly; while the less demonstrative Rosamund, with a look of curiosity and intense pain, but tearless eyes, is peering over the Queen's shoulder at the kneeling Melvil.

On the left of the maids and almost on a line with the Queen, the Earl of Leicester, who has all along been fickle, vacillating, loving Mary in secret but denouncing her to Queen Elizabeth, pressing his suit upon both queens secretly at intervals, at last stands resolute, burdened with grief, remorse, self-accusation, but erect, handsome, and dignified. A dark scowl contracts his brow, throwing his high and prominent forehead into still bolder relief, while his eyes are downcast and upon the loyal and kneeling steward. One hand reposes upon the hilt of his sword, whose point rests upon the stone floor, while the other hangs at his side. His tall form and fine manly bearing, added to his handsome features, which appear paler than otherwise in contrast with his raven black moustache and whiskers, bring him into relief as one of the four prominent characters of the word painting. A faithful and devoted page of the Earl has thrown himself in a paroxysm of grief upon his master, whom he holds by the shoulders with his head buried upon Leicester's breast.

In the distance, and on the extreme left is seen Margaret Curl, the Queen's attendant, who is approaching from her mistress's apartment, whither she remained to set it in order after she had prepared Mary for her walk to the scaffold.

A short way to the right of Hannah Kennedy, but at a respectful distance from the group, stands Sir Amias Paulet, the keeper of Mary, at the head of a guard of soldiers. He has his hands crossed upon the hilt of his sword—which reaches from his waist to the floor—resolute, obedient, conscientious, loyal, moved by Mary's sad condition, but unaffected by it to the extent of any evasion of duty which his royal mistress or her counsellors of state require to be done. He stands awaiting the termination of the leave-partings, when he is to conduct the doomed sovereign to the block.

In the foreground, is Lord Burleigh, through whose urgent persuasions Queen Elizabeth was prevailed upon finally to sign her royal cousin's death warrant. He is leaning against the balustrade at the head of the stone steps that lead to the fated cell below. His right hand is extended and points in the direction of the scaffold, while the other, which contains the death warrant, holds also his loose, handsomely embroidered garment gathered about his body. His face is turned to the group around Mary, and his stern, hard features indicate malignity, cinicism, satisfaction, gratification, as he sees the near prospect of the realization of his plans, intrigues, and misrepresentations to Queen Elizabeth, and at the same time anxiety lest some accident or mishap might yet intervene and prevent the carrying out of his sovereign's will. Hence his desire to terminate the farewell greetings, which he enjoys in a measure but regards sneeringly. His dark visage and sinister expressions appear still more repellant in contrast with the long white feather of his chapeau curling around his black luxuriant hair.

The arrangement of the personages in this word painting brings into prominent relief the four principal actors in the tragedy, Queen Mary, Melvil, Leicester, and Lord Burleigh.

At her execution she spurned the proposal to send the Dean of Peterborough, a Protestant, to attend her in the dying hour. After her death the Dean whilst her head was being held up to the gaze of the spectators said: "So perish all the Queen's enemies? She was buried in Westminster Abbey.

The King of Scotland her son, in hot vengeance, declared wrath against Elizabeth the murderer of his mother, but she wrote him letters of explanation and conciliation and so absorbed was he in the idea of the succession to Elizabeth's crown that the foul murder of his mother was passed unheeded by.

Thus passed away from earth, Marie Stuart a charming woman in mind, personal loveliness and conversation. Ambition ruined her and the breath of fanaticism soiled her young and ardent spirits. Let us close her melancholy career with the well known epitaph. "Requiescat in pace."

One of the great results of the death of Mary was the Armada, which occurred immediately after her execution at Fotheringay, and with which we close these sketches of Scottish History.

THE SPANISH ARMADA.

" In the year 1587, when Elizabeth sat on the throne, rumours were abroad of a mighty armament preparing by Philip II. of Spain for the invasion of England.

Early in the year 1588 the invader had completed his preparations. An armament was collected at Lisbon, the most formidable that had ever been launched on the sea. It received the name of *The Invincible Armada*, from the vain presumption that it could not be resisted. It consisted of 65 large ships of war, besides numerous vessels of smaller size,— in all 130 vessels, carrying 2431 pieces of artillery. The sailors and soldiers numbered 30,000, and, besides these, there were on board no fewer than 600 monks.

The Armada had been appointed to sail early in May, but was delayed by the death of the two principal commanders. At length it left Lisbon ; and, on Friday, July 19, its appearance off Lizard Point was announced at Plymouth, where the main squadron of the English fleet was stationed.

" Attend, all ye who list to hear our noble England's praise :
I sing of the thrice famous deeds she wrought in
  ancient days,
When that great fleet invincible against her bore,
  in vain,
The richest spoils of Mexico, the stoutest hearts
  in Spain.
It was about the lovely close of a warm summer's
  day,

There came a gallant merchant ship full sail to
  Plymouth Bay;
The crew had seen Castile's black fleet beyond
  Aurigny's Isle,
At earliest twilight, on the waves lie heaving
  many a mile.
At sunrise she escaped their van, by God's espe-
  cial grace;
And the tall Pinta till the noon had held her
  close in chase.
Forthwith a guard at every gun was placed along
  the wall;
The beacon blazed upon the roof of Edgecombe's
  lofty hall;
Many a light fishing-bark put out to pry along
  the coast;
And with loose rein and bloody spur rode inland
  many a post.

With his white hair unbonneted the stout old
  sheriff comes;
Behind him march the halberdiers, before him
  sound the drums.
The yeomen round the market-cross make clear
  an ample space,
For there behoves him to set up the standard of
  Her Grace:
And haughtily the trumpets peal, and gaily dance
  the bells,
As slow upon the labouring wind the royal blazon
  swells.
Look how the lion of the sea lifts up his ancient
  crown,

And underneath his deadly paws treads the gay
   lilies down!
So stalked he whan he turned to flight, on that
   famed Picard field,
Bohemia's plume and Genoa's bow and Cæsar's
   eagle shield:
So glared he when at Agincourt in wrath he turned to bay,
And crushed and torn beneath his claws the
   princely huuters lay.
Ho! strike the flagstaff deep, sir knight! Ho!
   scatter flowers, fair maids!
Ho, gunners! fire a loud salute! Ho, gallants!
   draw your blades!
Thou, sun, shine on her joyously! ye breezes,
   waft her wide!
Our glorious *semper eadem*—the banner of our
   pride!

The fresh'ning breeze of eve unfurled that banner's massy fold—
The parting gleam of sunshine kissed that haughty scroll of gold.
Night sunk upon the dusky beach and on the
   purple sea;
Such night in England ne'er had been, nor e'er
   again shall be.
From Eddystone to Berwick bounds, from Lynn
   to Milford Bay,
That time of slumber was as bright, as busy as
   the day;
For swift to east, and swift to west, the warning
   radiance spread—

High on St. Michael's Mount it shone—it shone on Beachy head.
Far o'er the deep the Spaniard saw, along each southern shire,
Cape beyond cape, in endless range, those twinkling points of fire.
The fisher left his skiff to rock on Tamar's glittering waves,
The rugged miners poured to war from Mendip's sunless caves :
O'er Longleat's towers, o'er Cranbourne's oaks, the fiery herald flew ;
He roused the shepherds of Stonehenge — the rangers of Beaulieu.
Right sharp and quick the bells rang out all night from Bristol town ;
And ere the day three hundred horse had met on Clifton Down
The sentinel on Whitehall gate looked forth into the night,
And saw, o'erhanging Richmond Hill, that streak of blood-red light.
The bugle's note and cannon's roar the death-like silence broke,
And with one start and with one cry the Royal City woke ;
At once, on all her stately gates, arose the answering fires ;
At once the wild alarum clashed from all her reeling spires ;
From all the batteries of the Tower pealed loud the voice of fear,
And all the thousand masts of Thames sent back a louder cheer ;

And from the furthest wards was heard the rush
 of hurrying feet,
And the broad streams of flags and pikes dashed
 down each rousing street;
And broader still became the blaze, and louder
 still the din,
As fast from every village round the horse came
 spurring in;
And eastward straight, for wild Blackheath, the
 warlike errand went;
And roused in many an ancient hall the gallant
 squires of Kent;
Southward, for Surrey's pleasant hills, flew those
 bright coursers forth;
High on black Hampstead's swarthy moor they
 started for the north;
And on, and on, without a pause, untired, they
 bounded still;
All night from tower to tower they sprang, all
 night from hill to hill;
Till the proud peak unfurled the flag o'er Derwent's rocky dales;
Till like volcanoes, flared to heaven the stormy
 hills of Wales;
Till twelve fair counties saw the blaze on Mal-
 vern's lonely height;
Till streamed in crimson on the wind the Wre-
 kin's crest of light;
Till broad and fierce the star came forth on Ely's
 stately fane,
And town and hamlet rose in arms o'er all the
 boundless plain;
Till Belvoir's lordly towers the sign to Lincoln
 sent,

And Lincoln sped the message on, o'er the wide
vale of Trent;
Till Skiddaw saw the fire that burnt on Gaunt's
embattled pile,
And the red glare on Skiddaw roused the burghers of Carlisle."

All England was roused. Vigorous preparations had for months before been making to resist the impending attack. The city of London, required to furnish 15 ships and 5000 men-at arms, placed double that number at the service of the Queen; and other wealthy towns imitated the generous patriotism of the capital. The Royal Navy had before consisted of only 30 vessels, but, by the united efforts of the government and the people, a fleet of 181 vessels was raised. None of them equalled those of the enemy in size, but they were under the command of more skilful seamen. Howard of Effingham was the Lord High Admiral; and under him were the celebrated naval commanders, Drake, Hawkins, and Frobisher.

Besides the fleet at Plymouth, an army of defence was posted at Tilbury on the Thames, under the orders of the Earl of Leicester. to oppose the invaders and protect the capital. Elizabeth visited the troops at Tilbury, rode on horseback along the lines, and delivered the following address to them: —" Let tyrants beware. 1 have always so behaved myself, that, under God, I have placed my chiefest strength and safeguard in the loyal hearts and good-will of my subjects; and, therefore, I am come amongst you, as you see, at this time, not for my own recreation and disport, but being resolved, in the midst, and heat of the battle, to live or die amongst you all,—to lay down, for my God, and for my kingdom, and for my people, my honour and my blood even in the dust. I know I have the body but of a weak and feeble woman, but I have the heart of a king, and of a king of England too; and I think foul scorn that Parma, or Spain, or any prince of Europe, should dare to invade the borders of my realm."

When the news came to Plymouth, the English fleet at once put to sea, and soon came in sight of the enemy, whose huge vessels were seen ploughing the waves in the form of a crescent, which extended about seven miles from one extremity to the other. The Spanish admiral did not attempt a landing on the southern coast, but steered directly up the Channel for the coast of Flanders; while Lord Howard, with his light vessels, maintained a running fire with great advantage against the colossal ships of the Spanish squadron.

On July 27 the great Armada came to anchor off Calais. Ten days afterwards the Spanish admiral advanced to Dunkirk, in order to clear the sea of the English fleet, and allow the Prince of Parma to embark an invading army. But in the middle of the night Lord Howard despatched a number of fire-ships against the Spanish fleet, and threw the entire Armada into confusion and dismay. Next day a general engagement took place. It lasted from four o'clock in the morning till six at night, and so disabled the mighty armament that the Spanish commander abandoned the enterprise; and, in order to save the remainder of his fleet, he resolved to return to Spain by circumnavigating the British Isles. He did not hazard a return by the English Channel. Want of ammunition prevented the conquerors from following him; but the elements rendered hostile operations wholly unnecessary. Soon after rounding the Orkney Islands a dreadful tempest arose, which ignorance of the seas and coasts rendered the more perilous. Horses, mules, artillery, and stores were thrown overboard, and the ships were scattered in all directions. Some were driven to the Norwegian shore, and stranded; others were wrecked on the Western Isles of Scotland; a few foundered with every soul on board; and upwards of thirty went to pieces on the coast of Ireland, near the Giant's Causeway. Towards the close of September the Spanish admiral reached Santander, in the Bay of Biscay, with a mere remnant of his force, the vessels shattered and the crews worn out.

Such was the issue of this memorable expedition, which cost Spain thousands of men and millions of money.

Elizabeth went in state to St. Paul's, to acknowledge the hand of Providence, which had been so visibly manifested in the signal deliverance of the country. A medal was struck bearing the appropriate inscription, "*Afflavit Deus et dissipantur*—God blew and they were scattered."

The dominion of the seas soon after this passed into the hands of Britain and she has ever since maintained her supremacy. May she continue to do so till the Archangel's blast declareth "Time shall be no more" and "Albion's Isle—*cum totam terram*,—be burned and parched and withered like to a scroll and a new Heaven and Earth arise from out the calcined ruins. "So mote it be."

CHAPTER XXV.

CONTENTS:

Continuation of the History of Scotland till the Union.—Queen Elizabeth's Death.—James Ist reign.—Charles I.—The Protector.—Charles II.—The Last Parliament and Union of Scotland and England.

"Concordia est Salus."
THE MONTREAL CITY MOTTO.

AT the solicitation of several friends who desire me to carry on the thread of Scotia's interesting History to the Union and leave off there, I will comply, in succinctly glancing at the principal items of information and importance from the Spanish Armada to the Union of Scotland and England in the person of James VIth.

When Queen Elizabeth placed her signature to the warrant for the execution of the young Earl of Essex she never enjoyed a day's happiness after. All her pleasures seemed to expire, she went about the business of the state mechanically and from the force of habit alone, her satisfactions and her pleasures were gone for ever,

This distress was enough to destroy her otherwise robust constitution and her end seemed rapidly approaching. Not long after, her voice left her and she fell into a lethargic slumber which continued some hours, but awaking, she addressed her courtiers in these words so often quoted now to show the utter worthliness of all sublunary things, " All my possessions for an inch of time" and gently expired without a groan in the seventieth year of her age and the forty-fifth of her reign. " *Sic transit gloria mundi.*"

Immediately on her demise 24th March 1603, Sir Robert Carey started from London to carry the news of the Queen's death to Edinburgh to King James. Fast and furious rode the knight (there were no railways or telegraphs then) night and day bravely on he rode and on Saturday night when the King had retired to bed, his horse's hoofs were heard clattering over the causeway of Edinburgh's High Street as down he rode to the Palace of Holyrood. He alighted there and was immediately ushered into the King's presence where at his bedside, kneeling down, he announced that his mistress Queen Elizabeth was dead, and saluted him as James the 1st of England. When three days after, he was proclaimed King of England, Scotland and Ireland, at the Cross of Edinburgh, there was a great blare of trumpets, singing and mighty cheering by all the people. It was exactly one hundred years before, when the stately Earl of Surry had delivered the beautiful English maiden into the hands of the Scottish barons, who became in time the great grand-mother of James VIth, and who was the first to mix the royal blood of Albion and Scotland in one commingling, and now James as the result, quietly stepped into the vacant throne of Queen Elizabeth of England.

Just as *his* only daughter, the Princess Elizabeth, married Frederick the Elector Palatine of the Rhine, from whom Our Most Gracious Majesty Queen Victoria descends and counts as having Stuart blood within her veins, so History repeats itself, for, from the time when Margaret Tudor the sister of Henry VIIIth wed the Scottish King, we look on, and see another English Princess brought to Bonnie Scotland as a Clansman's wife, in the person of H. R. Highness Princess Louise. And thus the countries are mixing MORE AND MORE and the time may come when all difference in religion, language and laws will be for ever swept away and Albion's Isle from Johnny Groat's House to Land's End be one in friendship, love and peace.

The History of King James' reign and that of his immediate successors belong principally to England and we will therefore only glance at the chief events therein. We may however state that if the Scotch like the Irish their brethren, were of captious dispositions, wishing for Home Rule and all its accessories the following from Mackenzie's History may well make them so, *even at the present hour.*

"The Scotch had small cause, in the first instance, to rejoice in the elevation of their king to the English throne. The loss of the court with its trappings and pageantries, which brought custom to the booths of the Edinburgh merchants and gave employment to the craftsmen, was severely felt. *Then the nobility and gentry followed the court to*

London, and spent there the incomes of their Scotch estates. The intercourse between the two countries was so small that the money never came back. It made matters worse that France, which had long favoured the Scotch by admitting their exports into French ports at trifling duties, now withdrew the preference, to the great injury of the trade of Scotland.

With her little trade thus sorely crippled, her court gone, and her money all flowing south, Scotland afforded no field for the enterprise of her sons. Great numbers of them left their native land to push for room and living in the world elsewhere. They repaired in such swarms to London, that the king had proclamation made at all the market-crosses of Scotland, forbidding any man to leave the country without a passport from the Privy Council. Many passed beyond the sea, and took service under foreign princes. A strong national brigade of Scots served under the banners of the celebrated Gustavus Adolphus, King of Sweden. Others entered the service of Austria, France, or the Italian States. Scots occasionally found themselves opposed to Scots in the continental wars, and sometimes a party of them, mounting a breach, would be hailed by a Scotch voice, "Come on; this is not like gallanting at the cross of Edinburgh!" Another numerous class of Scotsmen found an outlet as pedlars and petty traders in Germany and Poland. In those days, when all trading was done at fairs, the travelling merchant, who carried his goods on pack-horses, or bore his pack on his own back, was an important person. Scotch pedlars abounded all over the north of Europe, and carried on most of the inland trade. Cautious, frugal, and persevering, many of them returned to their native country with what enabled them to pass the rest of their lives in ease and comfort."

After the death of James, his son Charles I, ascended the throne, who considered that a King's mere will is above every law, but found himself mistaken. Charles visited Scotland like his father James. His insolence to his Parliament was almost unbounded. It was during his reign that the "Service Book" set all Scotland and England in commotion. Charles refused to make the least concession and then came the terrible days of the Cavaliers and Roundheads, and the battle of Marston Moor, etc. Charles died on the scaffold, the Martyr King as he has been called, and yet he was one who went against the wishes and advice of all his friends and people. He left his son Charles IInd, who was proclaimed in Scotland and who was a bigger blockhead than his father. *Vox populi* must prevail.

Between them reigned the Protector, fit title for the good he did. Oliver Cromwell was the people's man, yet even he outstepped his bounds; but all he did never could surpass the littleness and nothingness of Charles II, who burned the works of mighty Milton and George Buchanan because it is said they contained teachings that men are not born slaves. Add to all this, the sainted bones of Cromwell's aged mother were exhumed and thrown to the wind, and BLAKE,

"Where Blake and mighty Nelson fell"

the mightiest save Nelson of Britain's Ocean's Sons, Blake's body was exhumed by the Merry Monarch's order and thrown, with a hundred others into a heap in St. Margaret's Church yard. Small spite and petty envy, fit attendants of such a royal crew. Amongst all the high born personages, who perished in this reign, there were none so pure, none so good, none so loyal as the Marquis of Argyll; McKenzie thus speaks :

The Marquis of Argyll, noble old Christian patriot, first statesman of his age, wise and revered counsellor of the Covenanters in the stormy times of the first Charles, went to London to congratulate the king on his restoration. It was he who set the crown on the king's head at Scone. When Charles was informed that Argyll had come to wait upon him, with an angry stamp of his foot he ordered him to be carried prisoner to the Tower. From the Tower he was sent down to Scotland to undergo a mock trial before a packed Parliament. He was found guilty of treason, in having complied with the government of Cromwell. They took a vote, " Head or hang ?" and it carried " Head," the execution to be in two days. In prison the marquis said to his friends, " Shortly you will envy me who am got before you. Mind that I tell you ; my skill fails if you will not either suffer much or sin much." On the way to the scaffold, " I could die," he said, " like a Roman, but choose rather to die as a Christian." And never, perhaps, in any death-scene to be read of in history, did the power in which dying saints are more than conquerors shine forth, more serene and grand, than on the scaffold where Archibald, Marquis of Argyll, stooped his head to the loaded axe of the " maiden."

Let us pass over the intervening years to the Union of the countries. Black, dark and desolate draw we a veil over Dumclog, Rullion Green and Glencoe. Suffice it say that after years of persecution, bloodshed and oppression Scotland at last attained her freedom her religion and her laws and nothing can be more appropriate or words more grand than the closing lines of McKenzie's History of our own loved Caledonia.

A. D. 1706

" Look, then, at an ancient Scottish spectacle, to be seen this once, and then to vanish for ever. It is the Riding of the Parliament, or procession at the opening of its sittings. The long line of street from Holyrood up to the Parliament House is railed on both sides. Outside the rails, the street is lined with guards on foot and on horse. Along this railed and guarded avenue the procession comes, headed by trumpeters and pursuivants in quaint heraldic garb. The members of Parliament come riding two and two. The commissioners of burghs have each one lackey attending on foot; commissioners of shires have two. After them come the barons and viscounts, each having a gentleman to support his train, and three lackeys to attend. The earls follow next, each having his train-bearing gentleman and four lackeys. Then come more trumpeters, pursuivants, and heralds, followed by the Lion-king-at-arms with robe, chain, baton, and foot-mantle. Next follow the crown, the sceptre, the purse, and the royal commission, each carried by an earl. The Lord High

Commissioner comes after, with his pages and footmen. Six marquises, each with six lackeys, and four dukes, each with eight lackeys, follow the commissioner. A troop of horse guards bring up the rear and closes the procession. Such was the Riding of the Scotch Parliament, a picturesque, many-coloured show, on which many generations of the Edinburgh citizens had gazed, but which they now saw for the last time.

The last Scottish Parliament is sitting, then. Fiery Scottish eloquence blazes out; the debates are vehement, stormy, fierce. Eager crowds wait without, clamorously debating over again what is debated within. The city, which is crowded with strangers from all parts of the country, seems as if under military occupation. Strong bodies of troops mount guard in the different streets. A wild cheer or a deep yell of execration gives occasional expression to the passions of the mob. A carriage drives swiftly along the street towards the Parliament House. The mob recognise the owner, and follow him with volleys of stones and curses. People talk together with loud voice and vehement gestures. All work and business stand still. Such is the appearance of Edinburgh when Scotland's last Parliament is debating the treaty of union.

All over the country, the excitement is equally great. Every man's blood is at fever heat. Scotland with one voice is against the union; for if Scotland gives up her own government, what treatment may not her Church, her commerce, receive at the hands of that powerful sister who had shown herself so jealous and grasping! Is the independence bought with the blood of heroes to be given away to our ancient enemy ? The agitation shakes the kingdom to its remotest corner. But the Act of Union is safe to pass, and it passes—the votes of a large majority of the Parliament being duly bought with English gold.

On the 1st day of May, the Act, having been passed also in the English Parliament, came into operation. The two nations, which in the course of their history had fought with each other three hundred and fourteen battles, and slain of each other's subjects more than a million of men, were now one. Scotland thenceforward ceased to have a separate government, and her Parliament merged in the one Parliament of Great Britain. " There is the end of an old song," said Lord Seafield, the Chancellor, when the last formality was over, and the Scottish Parliament broke up for ever. Perhaps it was the saying of a man who affects indifference when his heart is heavy.

From the period of the Union, Scotland, amalgamated with England into one empire, ceases to have a separate history. She has enjoyed the vast advantage of being united with a great and powerful nation, and in the marvellous prosperity of the British Empire she has fully shared. Her imports of foreign merchandise have increased since the Union twenty-fold, her exports have increased forty-fold, and her revenue sixty-fold. Her agriculture is perhaps the best in the world. Her manufactures and the rich resources of her mineral wealth have been developed to a vast and splendid extent. The comforts and accommodations of life have increased beyond calculation. Little thatch-roofed towns, their streets soaking with filth, and lighted at night by the yellow glimmer of horn lanterns which the citizens were ordered to hang out, have grown into cities of palaces, where the brilliancy of gas turns night into day. Bridle-paths, deep in mire, winding over dreary breadths of moorland, have been changed into railroads; and the pack-horse, slow-plodding on his way, has given place to the steam-car. The carrier, as the organ of communication, has yielded up his business to the penny-post and the electric telegraph.

If Scotland shares in the prosperity and glory of Britain, Scotland may be permitted to say that she has contributed to both. The Scotchman, James Watt, and his steam-engine, have enabled Britain to manufacture for the world. The Scotchman, Adam Smith, taught Britain the great principle of free-trade, which is giving daily expansion to her commerce and increase to her wealth. Among the authors, the poets, the orators, the philosophers, whose genius has exalted the fame of our common country, the names of Scotchmen are not the meanest. And where is the region of the earth in which Scottish blood has not flowed to maintain the rights and the honor of Britain? The snows of Canada and the sands of Egypt, the fields of Spain and of India, have drunk it in. The ringing cheer of "Scotland for ever!" as the Greys galloped down the slope of Waterloo, told that the despot's hour was come. And who will ever forget the "thin red streak" at Balaclava, or the battle-march of Havelock's heroic men to the relief of Lucknow?

CHAPTER XXVI.

HISTORY OF THE HOUSE OF ARGYLL.

THE name of Argyll is derived from two Gaelic words *Earra Ghaidheal* or the country of the western Gael. Skene however says it is derived from *Oirirgael* that name by which the Highlanders call the ancient district of Argyll including Lochaber and Wester Ross. "In the middle ages the Macdougalls of Lorn held sway over Argyll and Mull whilst the Macdonalds, Lords of the Isles were supreme in Islay, Kintyre and the Southern Islands. The power of the Macdonalds was broken by Robert the Bruce and their estates bestowed on the Campbells, who originally belonged to the ancient earldom of Garmoran."

Campbell is a name of great antiquity in Scottish History and one of those most frequently mentioned. Pinkerton states that the name is derived from that of a Norman Knight named de Campo Bello. This Knight came to England in the train and with the army of William the Conqueror. This idea is supposed by other writers to be erroneous, as the name does not appear in the famous list of the Roll of Battle-Abbey, nevertheless such a Knight may have come over later in the reign of William Ist or of his son William IInd the Rufus.

In the oldest form of writing the name however is spelled Cambel or Kambel and is thus found in many ancient documents. This mode of spelling the word was generally adopted " by parties not acquainted with the individuals whose name they record," as it is certain that at every period, the family has always written the name CAMPBELL and "notwithstanding the extraordinary diversity that occurs in the spelling of other names by their holders, yet the invariable employment of the letter p by the Campbells themselves would be a strong argument for the southern origin of the name did there not exist in the record of the parliament of Robert Bruce in 1320 the name of the then head of the family, entered as Sir Nigel de Campo Bello."

There are several fabulous tales of the sennachies which are unnecessary to be treated of here. "According to the genealogists of the family of Argyll their predecessors on the female side were possessors of Lochow in Argyllshire as early as A. D. 404." In the eleventh century Gillespie or Archibald Campbell a gentleman of Anglo-Norman lineage, acquired these lands of Lochow by marriage with Eva, daughter of Paul O'Dwin, Lord of Lochow, who was otherwise called Paul Isporran, from his being the treasurer of the King. His son was called Duncan who lived in the reign of Malcolm IVth and left a son Colin who possessed the property in the reign of William the Lion. During the reign of Alexander Ist his son Gillespie or Archibald must have held 'Lochow as he is mentioned in the statutes of that King. His son Duncan married a daughter of the House of Comyn in the reign of the IInd Alexander whose son Sir Gillespie is mentioned in the times of Alexander IIIrd.

Sir Colin Campbell of Lochow distinguished himself during this King's reign and was Knighted by him in 1280. In 1291 he was one of the nominees on the part of Robert Bruce in the contest for the Scottish crown. He greatly added to his estates and hence received the name of MAC CHAILLAN MORE. More signifies great and Mac means son and therefore the whole name signifies *Colin the great chief*.

He quarrelled with a powerful neighbor the Lord of Lorne and in the feud was slain. This occasioned a series of bitter fights between the two houses of Lochow and Lorne, which were at last ended by the marriage of the daughter of Ergadia the Celtic proprietor of Lorne with John Stewart of Innermeath, 1386.

Sir Niel Campbell of Lochow, his eldest son, swore fealty to Edward Ist, but afterwards joined Robert the Bruce and fought bravely and like a worthy patriot as he was, by the side of his renowned master, in every battle, from that of Methven to the glorious victory of Bannockburn. The King rewarded his services by giving him in marriage *his own sister* Lady Mary Bruce. His next brother Donald is the progenitor of the race of the Campbells of Loudon.

After the death of Sir Niel, Sir Colin obtained a charter from his uncle King Robert Bruce of the lands of Lochow and Ardscodniche in which he is designated *Colinus filius Nigelli Cambel militis*. He died about 1340 and his eldest son Sir Gillespie or Archibald succeeded, who dying left the estates to his eldest son Sir Duncan. He was one of the hostages, under the name of Duncan, *Lord of Argyll*, for the sum of £40,000, for the expense of King

James Ist maintenance during his imprisonment in England. *Sir Duncan was the first who assumed the name of Argyll.* He died in 1453 and was buried at Kilmun. He had married Marjory or Mariota Stuart daughter of Robert, Duke of Albany, Governor of Scotland. He became a Lord of Parliament in 1445 under the title of *Lord Campbell, the first so called of this title.* He was succeeded by his grandson Colin, the son of his second son who had died before him. It was this Campbell who married the eldest daughter of John Stewart third Lord of Lorne and of Innermeath. In 1457 he was created *the first Earl of Argyll* and was also lord high Chancellor of Scotland. His wife Lady Isabella Stuart was the eldest of three sisters. The first Earl of Argyll having acquired the principal part of the landed property of his wife's sisters, then entered into a transaction with Walter Stewart, Lord of Lorne, their uncle to whom the Lordship of Lorne had descended by which he resigned the title and lordship of Lorne in favor of the Earl of Argyll who there upon added the style and designation of Lord Lorne to his other titles; being now called LORD CAMPBELL, THE EARL OF ARGYLL AND BARON OF LORNE. He died in 1493. His eldest son Archibald the second Earl was one of those who fell fighting around their King at Flodden's bloody field. He commanded the right wing of the Scottish army in that sanguinary day. His eldest son Colin thus became the third Earl. He was justice-general of Scotland. He accompanied the young King James Vth against the Queen mother and the rebel Lords and on the escape of the King in his 17th year from the power of the House of Douglas he was one of the very first to join his King at Stirling Castle. He fought against the Earl of Angus and compelled him to flee to England, and died 1530.

By his Countess Lady Jane Gordon he had three sons and a daughter. The eldest son Archibald became the fourth Earl of Argyll, 1530. He was appointed to all the offices which had been held by the former two Earls. *This Earl is memorable as the first of the Scots nobles who embraced the Reformation.* At the disastrous battle of Pinkie in 1547, the Earl of Argyll had the command of a large body of Highlanders. When the Queen Regent (Mary of Guise) proceeded to the north in 1556 to hold justice courts for the punishment of great offenders, the Earl of Argyll accompanied her. He died in 1558. He was twice married, 1st Lady Helen Hamilton; 2nd Lady Mary Graham. The son of Lady Hamilton became the fifth Earl, and the son of Lady Graham the sixth Earl.

Archibald the fifth Earl was educated by John Douglas his father's domestic Chaplain, who had been a Carmelite Friar but had embraced the Reformed Religion. He distinguished himself as one of the most able among the Lords of the Congregation. This Earl was one of them who went to Paris in order to crown Francis at his marriage with Queen Mary with the title of King of Scotland, but he was against her marrying Darnley, although subscribing for her marriage with Bothwell. After an eventful career, he died in September 1575. He had married Queen Mary's half-sister and died without issue, and was succeeded by his brother Colin sixth Earl of Argyll and who was also lord high Chancellor. This Earl on the 28th January 1581 with the King and many of the nobles subscribed *the second Confession of Faith.* After a long illness he died in 1584. He was twice married, 1st Janet, eldest daughter of Lord Methven, no issue, and 2d Lady Agnes Keith whose eldest son became Archibald seventh Earl of Argyll. He was a minor when his father died.

In 1592 when little more than 16 years of age he married Lady Anne Douglas. When the decreet of ranking the Scots' nobility in 1606 was issued the Earl of Argyll was placed second on the list of Earls. His first Countess having died, he married Anne, daughter of Sir William Cornwall. This lady was a zealous Roman Catholic and although the Earl was a warm Protestant she gradually drew him over to profess the same faith as herself. By Lady Anne Douglas he had a son who became Archibald eighth Earl of Argyll. He died in London in 1638.

Archibald Campbell the eighth Earl an eminent patriot was created in 1641, *the first Marquis of Argyll.* He attended the general assembly held at Glasgow. This Earl had the principal hand in bringing Charles II to Scotland during the times of Charles II and Cromwell. He played an important part, but was at last condemned to be executed.

He was beheaded, by the Maiden a kind of guillotine, at the Cross of Edinburgh, May 27th 1661. On the sentence being pronounced the Marquis said " I had the honor to set the crown upon the King's head and now he hastens me to a better crown than his own." By his wife Lady Margaret Douglas he had two sons and three daughters. His eldest son became Archibald ninth Earl of Argyll and second Marquis. He was educated in the true principles of loyalty and the Protestant religion by his father. Like his father he fell into difficulty with the government and being confined in Edinburgh, was at last beheaded by the Maiden June 30th 1685. He was twice married; 1st Lady Mary Stuart and 2nd Lady Anne Mackenzie. His eldest son Archibald Campbell became the tenth Earl, the third Marquis and *the first who bore the title of* DUKE OF ARGYLL. He was created Duke in 1701, was an active promoter of the Revolution. He also accompanied the Prince of Orange to England. He was one of the Scots commissioners who were deputed to offer the crown of Scotland to " William of pious memory," and to tender him the coronation oath. For this and other eminent services the family estates which had been forfeited were restored to him. On the 23rd June 1701 he was created by letters patent DUKE OF ARGYLL, *Marquis of Lorne and Kintyre, Earl of Campbell, Viscount of Lochow and Baron Inverary.* He married Elizabeth daughter of Sir Lionel Talmash and left two sons, the elder becoming the celebrated John, Duke of Argyll. He died in 1703.

John Campbell, the second Duke, who was also created Duke of Greenwich, was the martial hero of the House of Campbell or Argyll. On the very day in which his grand-father was beheaded he fell from a window of an upper room of Lethington, then the seat of his grand-mother the Duchess of Lauderdale, and received no injury. When seventeen years of age, his father introduced him to King William who gave him the command of a regiment. Nine years after on the death of his father he became Duke of Argyll. When the order of the Thistle was revived in 1704, he was installed one of the Knights of that order. Being sent to Scotland relative to the Union he became very unpopular there. In 1706, his Grace fought in Flanders under the great Marlborough and distinguished himself at the battle of Ramillies and at the siege of Ostend, as also at the attack of Meenen. In 1708 he commanded 20 battalions at the famous battle of Oudenarde and took a considerable share in the victory of Malplaquet. When George the first arrived in England he was made general and commander-in-chief of the King's forces in Scotland. He was also afterwards made Field Marshal.

The Rebellion broke out in 1715. The Duke of Argyll then defeated the army of the Earl of Mar at Sheriffmuir and forced the Pretender to retire from Scotland. He passed through many viscissitudes, being several times deprived of his offices and again having them restored. This amiable and highly accomplished nobleman has been immortalized by Pope in the lines:

" Argyll, the state's whole thunder born to wield
And shake alike the senate and the field."

The celebrated Scottish Poet, Thomson, the author of "The Seasons," in Winter introduces an encomium on his Grace, and he is also mentioned by Tickell, Broome and other poets of his time. The lines of Thomson are the following:

"Yes, there are such. And full on thee, *Argyll*,
Her hope, her stay, her darling, and her boast,
From the first *patriots* and her heroes sprung,
Thy fond imploring country turns her eye;
In thee, with all a mother's triumph, sees
Her every virtue, every grace combin'd;
Her genius, wisdom, her engaging turn;
Her pride of honour, and her courage tried,
Calm and intrepid, in the very throat
Of sulph'rous war, on Tenier's dreadful field.
*Nor less the palm of peace inwreaths thy brow;
For, powerful as thy sword,* from thy rich tongue
Persuasion flows, and wins the high debate;
While mix'd in thee combine the charm of youth,
The force of manhood, and the depth of age.
Thee, Forbes, too, whom every worth attends,
As truths sincere, as weeping friendship kind;
Thee, truly generous, and in silence great,
Thy country feels thro' her reviving arts,
Plann'd by thy wisdom, by thy soul inform'd;
And seldom has she known a friend like thee."

He was twice married, 1st Mary Brown and 2nd Jane Warburton. He left no son but five daughters by his second wife and thus his English titles at his death in 1743. became extinct whilst the Argyll estates passed into the hands of his brother Archibald, third Duke of Argyll.

This short sketch of the great Duke of Argyll would be incomplete without inserting the well known song made on his Grace during the stirring period of 1715. Every one knows the song and air.

THE CAMPBELLS ARE COMING.

Upon the Lomonds I lay, I lay,
Upon the Lomonds I lay, I lay;
I looked down to bonnie Lochleven,
And saw three bonnie perches play.

The Campbells are comin', O ho, O ho,
The Campbells are comin', O ho, O ho,
The Campbells are comin' to bonnie Lochleven,
The Campbells are comin', O ho, O ho.

The great Argyll, he goes before,
He makes the canons and guns to roar:
Wi' sound o' trumpet, pipe and drum,
The Campbells are comin', O ho, O ho.

The Campbells are comin', O ho, O ho,
The Campbells are comin', O ho, O ho,
The Campbells are comin' to bonnie Lochleven,
The Campbells are comin', O ho, O ho.

The Campbells they are a' in arms,
Their loyal faith and truth to show;
Wi' banners rattlin' in the wind,
The Campbells are comin', O ho, O ho.

The Campbells are comin', O ho, O ho,
The Campbells are comin' O ho, O ho;
The Campbells are comin' to bonnie Lochleven,
The Campbells are comin', O ho, O ho.

Archibald the third Duke was also under General Marlborough, but soon abandoned the military profession and employed himself in acquiring those qualifications necessary for a statesman. He fought for the King during the rebellion of 1715 and was wounded at Sheriffmuir. *This Duke built the beautiful Castle of Inverary* and collected one of the most valuable private libraries in Great Britain. He died suddenly while sitting in his chair at dinner, April 15th 1761. He had married a daughter of Mr. Whitfield, pay master of Marines, but had no children. The title then descended to his cousin, John, fourth Duke, son of the Hon. John Campbell of Mamore, the second son of Archibald, the ninth Earl of Argyll, he who was beheaded in 1685. He also was in the army and acted as aide-de-camp to his chief "The Great Argyll." When he succeeded to the title he was chosen one of the sixteen representative peers of Scotland. He died in 1770 in the 77th year of his age. He married the Hon. Mary Bellenden and had four sons and a daughter. His eldest son John succeeded him as fifth Duke of Argyll in 1770. This Duke was chosen the first President of the Highland Society of Scotland, to which Society, his Grace generously donated the handsome sum of £1,000 sterling as the beginning of a fund for educating young men of the West Highlands for the Navy. He had married in 1759 Elizabeth, widow of James, sixth Duke of Hamilton. His family consisted of three sons and two daughters: 1. George John, Earl of Campbell, who died in infancy; 2. George William, Marquis of Lorne, and who became the sixth Duke of Argyll; 3. John Douglas Edward Henry, who became the seventh Duke of Argyll, and Lady Augusta and

Lady Charlotte Susan Maria who is styled "The Flower of the House of Argyll." She was the Authoress of several novels. The Duke died 24th May 1806 in the 83rd year of his age.

George William his son succeeded as the sixth Duke. He was appointed vice-admiral over the western coasts and islands of Scotland. He married 1810, Caroline Elizabeth, daughter of the fourth Earl of Jersey, and died October 1839 without issue.

His brother, John Douglas Edward Henry, succeeded as seventh Duke. This Duke was no less than three times married, 1st to Elizabeth Campbell of Fairfield, who died in 1818; 2nd to Joan Glassel of Long Niddry, and 3rd to Anne Colquhoun Cunningham of Craigends. His second wife bore him two sons and one daughter. The first son, John Henry died when in his sixteenth year, his second, George Douglas, Marquis of Lorne succeeded as the present or eighth Duke of Argyll. His Grace died A. D. 1847.

George Douglas Campbell, the eighth Duke, the present worthy representative of the ancient House was born in 1823. He is not only an Author of no mean fame but a distinguished orator and statesman. Long before he came to the dukedom of Argyll, he took a prominent part in the controversy then raging throughout Scotland in connection with patronage and ended in joining the side of the celebrated Dr. Chalmers. In 1842, when only nineteen years of age he issued a pamphlet entitled "A Letter to the Peers from a Peer's son." Several others followed, chief of which perhaps is that entitled "An

Essay on the Ecclesiastical History of Scotland since the Reformation. In 1848, he published an essay called: "Presbytery Examined." His last work, 1878, on the Eastern Question, has had so rapid a sale that the publishers cannot supply the demand.

He was elected Chancellor of St. Andrew's University, 1851, Lord Privy Seal, 1853-5; Postmaster General, 1855-8; Knight of the Thistle 1856 and again Lord Privy Seal 1859. He was also for two years 1854 and 1855, Chancellor of the University of Glasgow. In 1861 he was elected President of the Royal Society of Edinburgh. He is also a Fellow of the Royal Society and an L.L.D.

When the Gladstone government came into power, his Grace accepted the position of Secretary of State for India in the duties of which department he was ably seconded and assisted by his eldest son, the Marquis of Lorne.

The Duke of Argyll married in 1844, Lady Elizabeth Georgiana Sutherland Leveson-Gower, the eldest daughter of the second Duke of Sutherland and late Mistress of the Robes to her Majesty the Queen. When she died, she was universally regretted by all who knew her as one of the most Christian and benevolent woman in Great Britain and bearing somewhat a strong resemblance to our Most Gracious Majesty, in her acts of goodness and sympathy to her fellow creatures. God blessed this union in a remarkable degree, the Duke and Duchess having no less than five sons and seven daughters, of whom the Marquis of Lorne, the eldest and heir apparent to the Dukedom, is now, with his

Illustrious Consort, in Canada, as the Governor General.

This sketch would be incomplete without inserting short biographical notices of the present occupants of Rideau Hall or Government House, Ottawa.

THE MARQUIS OF LORNE, John George Edward Henry Douglas Sutherland Campbell, M.P. for his native county, before he came to Canada, is the eldest son of the eighth and present Duke of Argyll. He was born A. D. 1845 and educated at Eton and Trinity College, Cambridge.

Every one remembers our beloved Queen's description of her future son-in-law when in "*Our Life in the Highlands*" she thus speaks of her reception at the old Castle of Inverary. " Our reception was in the true Highland fashion. The pipers walked before the carriage and the Highlanders on either side, as we approached the house. Outside stood the Marquis of Lorne, just two years old, a dear, white, fat, fair little fellow, with reddish hair, but very delicate features like both his father and mother; he is such a merry independent little child. He had a black velvet dress and jacket, with a "Sporran" scarf, and "Highland bonnet."

His Excellency in 1866 was appointed a Captain in the London Scottish Volunteers and in 1869, in the Sutherlandshire Rifles.

He is a zealous supporter of the volunteer movement, and is a practised marksman with the rifle. He has shot with success in the University vs. House of Lords and Commons' matches at Wimbledon. He undertook, whilst Private Secretary to his father in the office of Secretary of State for India, and carried on with assiduity and success, an amount of business not usually within the sphere nor the ordinary capacity of a private secretary. When he returned from a visit to the United States he published an interesting volume called "A Trip to the Tropics" " a creditable production when the extreme youth and aristocratic education of the writer are taken into consideration," thus writes an editorial critic.

But the greatest event in the life of the Marquis of Lorne is his propitious marriage with Her Royal Highness the Princess Louise, the fourth daughter of Our Most Gracious Majesty the Queen.

H. R. H. PRINCESS LOUISE, was born at Buckingham Palace 18th May 1848. She is highly accomplished in drawing, painting, but especially sculpture. The bust of Her Majesty, her Mother in the Royal Academy Exhibition of 1870 "possessed real merits of execution and verisimilitude." When the news of the intended marriage of the Marquis of Lorne and the Princess Louise was made public, a vast amount of congratulation succeeded in every circle of every dependency of the British Empire, as well as throughout Great Britain. The peculiarity of this marriage was the theme on every tongue. A subject, though that subject, one of the highest of the realm, to become the husband of one of the Royal Princesses, this was indeed, the breaking down of old conventualities and almost adamantine usage. For five hundred years previous in the History of England no Princess had been allowed to marry a subject of the reigning house. Princes have occasionally broken through this law, but of the Royal Princesses, *never one;* not one single instance is there on record since the days of Edward IIIrd, five hundred years ago. There have been four or five instances of princesses marrying subjects, but these have all been under peculiar circumstances and some of them never fully recognized. "It is a well known fact that during the past hundred years the marriage of Royalty with a subject has been illegal, except the royal personage intending to contract such a marriage has received for it the special sanction of the Sovereign." "It is impossible then, not to admire the courage of Her Majesty in putting aside precedents, which were thus enforced by some of her predecessors without any consideration for the feelings of those immediately affected by them. The Queen has preferred the happiness of her daughter to a pedantic adherence at variance with popular feeling and which now ceased to be supported by any weight of reason."

And now in March 1871, the highest and most exalted of all the brides of the House of Argyll, stands before the altar to become the wife of the future MacCaillan More. In the words of the "*Court Journal.*" " Having arrived at the altar the group is formed. Though the voice of the good Bishop (the Bishop of London) is plainly audible and we see Her Majesty's movement of assent that she gives the Princess away, nothing more is heard; and we rather extol the depriving us of the pleasure of a loud response, for when two fond hearts pledge themselves as they do undoubtedly here, to our thinking the natural tone is love's whisper. And now 'tis done, and John Douglas Sutherland and Louise Caroline Alberta (as they were named by the Bishop in the ceremony) are one." "The Princess embraces her mother and the Marquis kneels and kisses the Queen's hand and the ceremony is complete."

This sketch would be incomplete without the two songs made on this auspicious occasion, one from the pen of a Canadian Author, Evan McColl, of Kingston, the other from the Poetess F. R. Havergal, lately dead. With these we conclude these "Sketches of Scottish History," and reiterate again what we wished in the Dedication at the commencement of these Sketches, that God will long bless and prosper them both in " Health, Wealth and Estate."

I

LOUISE.

Hurrah! for the news o'er the wide world just
    gone out!
The bards all enraptured are rhyming upon it:
A son of the Mist (up yet higher my bonnet!)
    Has won the young heart of Balmoral's Louise.
Glad tidings to all save those wee German lairdies
Whose wont was to steal our choice flowers for
    their " yairdies."
Hence forth, from such theft let's pray Cupid to
    guard us,
    And give a gay Lorne to each charming Louise.

'Tis long since the Gael of both mainland and island
Well knew that in heart the dear lassie was Highland,
The Stuart, it seemed, with a strip o' Argyll in't,
   Would just be the plaid to suit winsome Louise!
Though earth's proudest King might right glad be to wed her,
She's much better match'd—thanks to love mang the heather!
A lad who can sport the MacCailean's proud feather
   Is just the right mate for the bonny Louise!

A gathering of Clans on my vision is looming,
Dunchuaich proudly echoes "The Campbells are coming!"
In fancy I listen the *Gunna Cam* booming
   Its joy at the Bridal of Lorne and Louise.
Alas that in fancy alone can I wend there
My welcome to give them—my homage to tender,
And help happy thousands the welkin to rend there,
   Proud toasting Lord Lorne and the Lady Louise.

II

SCOTLAND'S WELCOME.

Sweet rose of the south, contented to rest
In the fair island home which thy presence has blessed,
From the Highlands resounding glad welcome shall float,
And the Lowlands re-echo the jubilant note.

Merry England has loved thee and cherished thee
   long,
Her blessings go with thee in prayer and in song;
Bonnie Scotland has won thee, and lays at thy feet
Love tender and fervent, love loyal and sweet.

Chorus.—Our own bonnie Scotland with welcome
      shall ring,
   While greeting and homage we loyally
      bring;
   The crown of our love shall thy diadem be,
   And the throne of our hearts is waiting
      for thee.

Then come like the summer that gilds with a smile
The dark mountains and valleys of lonely Argyll,
Golden splendour shall fall on the pale northern
   snow
And with rose-light of love, the purple shall glow.
Though the voice that should bless, and the hand
   that should seal,
Are away and at rest in the " Land o' the leal,"
May the God of thy Father look graciously down
With blessings on blessings thy gladness to crown.

Chorus.--Our own bonnie Scotland with welcome
      shall ring,
   While greeting and homage we loyally
      bring,
   The crown of our love shall thy diadem be,
   And the throne of our hearts is waiting
      for thee.

FUGITIVE PIECES

BY

Revd. John Douglas Borthwick,

Written on various occasions in the later History of Great Britain.

FAREWELL TO SCOTLAND.

ON LEAVING SCOTLAND, MAY 1850, FOR CANADA.

The hour is come and I obey—
  I leave my native land;
And grief sits heavy on my heart
  At parting, Scotia's strand,
And must I never see my home,
  My father, mother true?
And must I o'er the ocean roam,
  And sob a last adieu?

And shall I never more return
  To Caledonia's shore?
Or breathe again the bracing breeze,
  Or see the winter's boar?
Or climb the mountain's steep, steep side,
  Or wander down the dell,
Or pull the primrose or the thyme,
  The fern or heather bell?

These scenes shall pass, but never fade—
  They're graven on my heart;
And till my blood shall curdle cold
  Shall never more depart;

Farewell, my own dear native land!
    Land of the brave and true;
Night closes o'er thy sea girt strand—
    Farewell, farewell—adieu!

One gaze—one long and sorrowing gaze—
    The last, that I shall see
Of thy wild shore and ruggèd strand—
    Thou land of liberty;
One gaze—my heart is heaving wild—
    My grief I cannot tell;
Scotia! a loyal, mountain child
    Bids thee for aye, farewell.

Charge of the Heavy and Light Brigades of British Cavalry at Balaklava, Oct. 23, 1854.

Charge of the Heavy Brigade.

I

The Russians stood, *en masse* below,
Lancers and Cossacks, all were there—
Eight thousand men and horse—to throw
The British camp and works to air:
Eight thousand men well armed and drill'd,
Whose chieftain's words each bosom thrill'd;
And to oppose their further way,
Were Enniskillen and Scot's Grey;
These regiments, in number few,

Had fought and bled at Waterloo;
Now side by side again they stood,
Again to dare a desperate feud,—
To die or gain the victory!

II

The bugle sounds, the war steeds neigh,
Their riders, burning are as they;
The word is given—" Charge !"—and they go
Like lightning on the hated foe;
And when they near the enemy,
Each soldier waves his sabre high,
And shouts for Albion's victory.

III

They dash like heroes thro' the rank,
Then many a brave dragoon soon sank,
Surrounded, hemm'd by hated foes,
That little band still bravely goes—
Still battles with superior might,
And closes in a desperate fight!
As bursts the moon from dark'ning cloud,
As bursts the sun from rainy shroud,
So the Red Coats appear once more,
Spatter'd and stain'd with Russian gore:
Gauntlets once white now red with blood,
And in each hand the dripping sword;
Once more the heroic band appeared
Once more for Albion's Queen they cheer'd,
And drove the Russian horse to flight;
But many a brave and gallant wight
That day met death and victory.

Charge of the Light Brigade.

I

Meanwhile the Light Division stood,
Weary to whet their swords in blood,
When Nolan, then to them convey'd
The word—Advance!—and well obey'd,
These gallant men, their falchions drew;
Each griped his sabre.—To their view
Three batteries appear'd—whose fire
Dealt death to all around;
But on the brave division goes,
Tho' scores fall to the ground;
They reach the guns, and at their side
Cut down the gunners, who're denied
The chance of flight—so rapidly
Has Albion's sons gained victory.

II

Like Alpine avalanche of snow
Which thunders to the vale below,
So rush the Light Dragoons to death,
To gain fair fame's immortal wreath,
Like snows which melt before the sun,
When spring arrives and winter's gone,
So Russians feel their arm of power,
And under British sabres cower;
Advance—retire—then flee apace,
Pursued by Albion's chivalry.

III

Scarce half remain'd, when all was done;
There, many a brave, heroic son

Of Albion's Isle, in prime of life,
Pour'd out his blood in fearful strife;
And when from that fierce charge return'd
Comrade for comrade slain, then mourn'd,
Stern in their death, those sons of fame
Have gain'd a fair, immortal name,
The glorious name of Victory.

IV

When years are past, and tears are dry,
How many, with a heavy sign
Shall feel the want of him that day
Who fell in Balaklava's fray!
And from the eye of beauty rare
Did flow the sad and briny tear,
When that long fatal list was seen
Of those who fell for Albion's Queen;
And long, for many years, the weeds
Shall tell of fierce and desperate deeds,
Perform'd by Britain's sons of fame,
For Balaklava's bloody name
Surrounds their brow with victory.

Mount Pleasant, C. W., 23 Oct. 1855.

THE PRINCE OF WALES.—Oct. 1860.

Royal Son, of much loved Monarch,
    High-born heir of high degree;
Heir to Britain's mighty empire,
    Prince of Wales—all welcomed thee.

Great thy nation—great thy sires,
  Noble Mother, good and true,
Royal Boy—in coming future
  May *her* goodness shine in *you*.

Empire's every hope and joy,
  Every subjects earnest prayer;
May thy after be a blessing,
  Britain's Pride and Britain's Heir.

In old Terra Prima Vista,
  By its rivers, lakes and sea,
By its shores, its forests, streamlets,
  Prince of Wales—all welcomed thee.

By Acadia's misty coasts,
  In Acadia's royal see;
By its forests, lakes and rivers,
  Prince of Wales—all welcomed thee.

Up the Gulf, and in the River,
  By men of high and low degree,
In the village, cot, and city,
  Prince of Wales—all welcomed thee.

Grand ovation, through the country,
  Great delight and revelrie,
Arches, speeches, triumphs, dances,
  Prince of Wales—all welcomed thee.

And when again on Albion's shore
  Thy hand shall clasp the Royal band;
In after years think of that time,
  Thy visit to this far off land.
And long may Canada to HER remain
  The Brightest Star in Britain's diadem.

ST. ANDREW'S DAY.

TO SCOTLAND.

I

William Wallace and Bruce,
The Douglas and Graham,
Randolf, Murray and Lovet,
These are thy names,
Names of heroic sons
In the days of yore
Names that are " Household Words"
From mountain to shore.

II

Lord Clyde and Napier,
Scott, Campbell and Burns,
And a long list of worthies,
To my memory returns,
As sitting, an exile,
And dropping a tear,
I think of Auld Scotia
On *this* day of the year.

III

Never more save in vision,
Shall I ever behold
The land of my forefathers,
Thou Land of the bold,
But may plenty surround thee,
Peace for ever be thine;
And thy glory and progress
For evermore shine.

IV

May the glorious old motto
Of the Thistle and Scot,
Be first in each front rank
And never forgot,
May the flag of St. Andrew
For ever be free,
And with St. George and St. Patrick's
Wave over each sea.

Montreal, 30 Nov. 1868.

THE 93rd HIGHLANDERS AT BALACLAVA.

25th October 1854.

I

Never since the days of Chivalry,
   Or the age of old Romance,
Or the times of the Knights-errant,
   On the sunny shores of France;
Never since the days of Douglas,
   Has such valor e'er been seen;
Since the days of Bruce and Wallace
   Or Scotia's martyr'd Queen;
As when these Highland heroes
   Fell, with such thundering crash,
On the soldiers of the Muscovite
   Like glance of lightning's flash.

II

Look at that glorious red line
   Of plumed and kilted Gael,

Descendants of Old Caledon,
  Whose falchions never fail;
See upon them, madly rushes
  Russian Pandour and Hussar,
Muscovite Dragoon and Lancer
  In the pageantry of war,
The silence is oppressive,
  But, between the cannon's roar,
The champing of the chargers' bits
  Is heard on th' Euxine shore,
And the well known clink of sabre
  Of Enniskillen and Scots Grey,
Is heard adown the valley
  Making ready for the fray.

III

For a moment do the Russians
  Halt—as in fear and dread
Then in one grand line of battle,
  Through the valley, fast they sped,
Spur to their utmost speed,
  Their chargers, on the way,
And gath'ring strength at ev'ry stride
  They hope to win the day,
In the war shout of the Muscovite
  They rush upon the Gael,
That thin red streak of Highlanders
  Topped with its line of steel.

IV

But when within three hundred yards,
  The front steel line goes down,

Then the Minnie musketry rings out,
  And the Scottish old renown,
And the chivalry of Caledon,
  And the true aim of her sons,
Are seen in emptied saddles
  And heard in shouts and groans,
In the terror of the Muscovite,
  As they wheel and open file,
And flee, both to the left and right,
  And leave that splendid Highland line
Untouched in all its might:
  Whilst the brave Sir Colin Campbell,
To the question makes reply,
  That the *well known British line two-deep*,
Was sufficient, with HIS Highlanders,
  To make the Russians fly.

V

Long may the glorious war deeds
  Of Scotia's sons be sung;
Till swords be beat to ploughshares
  And in peaceful halls, be hung
The trumpet and the clarion,—
  And war be learned no more,
But the blessings of Christ's Gospel
  Be felt from shore to shore,
When throughout the wide, wide world
  Shall be Angelic Peace,
And war, with all its miseries,
  For evermore shall cease.

Montreal, Oct. 1871.

APPENDIX.

The name of Borthwick has been so intimately connected with these Sketches, that the following from the "London World"—of August 6th 1879—will be read with interest. The "Morning Post" of London, England, is the paper that is mentioned in this article and is, we believe, owned by Mr. Borthwick, father of the Borthwick of Napoleon's *coup d'Etat.*

NAPOLEON AND THE COUP D'ETAT.

A NEW VIEW OF THE 2ND DECEMBER, BY A BRITISH JOURNALIST WHO WAS BEHIND THE SCENES.

Mr. Borthwick's father—the head of the Borthwicks of Glencorse, collaterals of Lord Borthwick's family—was one of those enthusiasts in politics who spend their substance freely on elections without extracting any *quid pro quo* from their party. With the Borthwicks this policy was traditional. They appear to have been rather loyal than astute politicians, and to have suffered accordingly. When fighting was to the fore, they had an odd habit of taking the losing side. Thus one head of the family was killed at Flodden; another came to grief under Mary Stuart, in consequence of a too warm espousal of her cause; a third was the original of Henry Morton, the hero of *Old Mortality.* It was not, it will be recollected, that Borthwick, *alias* Henry Morton, loved the Covenauters—on the contrary, he abhorred them—but his sense of the duties of hospitality was exalted as that of Ruy Gomez de Silva. In later times the Borthwicks clung to the Stuarts and lost their estates, but after all the misfortunes of his family the member for Evesham had a handsome income when he came of age, and his son naturally expected a political career like his distinguished father, whose chief opponent in the House, Mr. Villiers—" Free-trade Villiers," the member for Wolverhampton—always speaks in the highest terms of his power as a parliamentary orator. The member for Evesham was one of the Young England party with the late Earl Strangford, Lord George Bentinck and Mr. Baillie Cochrane, a thorough-paced Tory and Protectionist, clinging to the idea that free trade and protection are not matters of principle, but of expediency; and having *more majorum*, got well on the losing side, clung to it with all the chivalrous loyalty of his race. The effect of this devotion to party was that when Mr. Algernon Borthwick reached the age of nineteen he found himself a gentleman without estate or the hope of one. Trained for diplomacy, and promised a nomination in the Foreign Office by Lord Aberdeen, he at once gave up his promised career and applied himself to journalism. He was very young ; but his training had been special. Educated partly in England and partly abroad, and having helped his father for some three years as secretary and *précis* writer, he had what may be called the run of politics and knew personally all the principal Englishmen of both parties. So far he had some stock-in-trade, but it was to be curiously applied, for his first essay in journalism was as Paris correspondent of the *Morning Post,* in which his father had some interest. Young Borthwick went to Paris, and going to work at once, soon acquired the art of combining and expressing the news which his father's friends and political connections enabled him to acquire. He had known the Prince President since he was a child, and was therefore on good terms at the Elysée, while Lady Normanby and the Duchesse de Grammont made every *salon* in Paris open its doors to him.

Over a quiet cigarette he will sometimes give his version of the *coup d'état*, a story quaint enough when contrasted with the many other extant versions of that celebrated event. According to Mr. Borthwick's reading, supported by not a few present in Paris at the end of November, 1851, nothing was less a secret than the contemplated move of the Prince President and the generals. Over all Paris hung the gloom of expectation. The precise form of action to be undertaken by the head of the Executive was of course unknown, but that something would be done was obvious. Napoleon had spoken of the Chamber as a *foyer de conspiration*, and had just written a pamphlet which put his views clearly before the public. This remarkable *brochure* was already scarce on the night of Monday, the 1st of December, and Mrs. Norton came to the Elysée in quest of one. The President had not a single copy left, and Lord Normanby had sent his to London, when young Borthwick said he would give the lady with the Irish eyes his copy if she would ask him to breakfast on the following morning. Mrs. Norton agreed, and then took her leave of Napoleon, saying that she must leave Paris. He protested against her departure, whereat she said, " Nothing would induce me to stay unless you promise me your *coup d'état.*" At these words he turned away, and a few minutes later at his usual hour, eleven o'clock, he withdrew. The Paris correspondent of the *Post* walked home by moonlight and slept soundly till his servant awakened him with the news that the *coup d'état* was struck. After telegraphing the news and the text of the proclamations to London, Mr. Borthwick went to Mrs. Norton's for his breakfast, and, thanks to her, saw most of the remarkable scenes of the 2nd December. Every quarter was occupied by troops, and it was impossible for a man to pass from one to the other. The presence of Mrs. Norton, however, made everything possible. The most obdurate yielded to the pleading of her beautiful eyes, and one cordon of troops was passed after another. Passing by the quays, the pair at last reached the Chamber, and witnessed the odd scene of the Deputies trying to get into their own house, and heard La Rochejaquelin deliver his harangue. On attempting to cross the Carrousel they found the " *On ne passe pas,*" very firmly uttered ; but after some expostulation, the sentry agreed to fetch his officer, who yielded to the irresistible eyes, and sent their owner and her companion across the great square with a corporal's guard. Thus they saw the Congress of Plumes, the great meeting of Bonapartist generals, convened by the Minister of War, St. Armand and General Fleury.

With two other individuals of this name we close. The first, David Borthwick of Lockhill, is remarkable as being a learned Lawyer and Judge. He was Lord Advocate of Scotland, in the reign of James the VIth, the first who ever bore the title. During the reign of Queen Mary, he, in May 1567, as Counsel for the Earl of Bothwell, took instruments of her pardon and forgiveness of him and his accomplices, for her abduction to Dunbar. He had acquired considerable lands in the shires of Berwick, Haddington and Fife, previous to his death in 1581. His son, to whom he had unconditionally given some of them, was a spendthrift and had to sell the property. This induced the old gentleman on his death-bed to exclaim bitterly : " What shall I say ? I give him to the devil that doth get a fool, and maketh not a fool of him."—This saying afterwards became a proverb and was called " David Borthwick's Testament.

The second, James Borthwick of Stow, practised as a physician in Edinburgh. He was a cadet of the Crookston family already spoken about, as descended from the second son of the first Lord Borthwick, who was called John de Borthwick. This gentleman deserves notice, as through his means the disjunction of the corporation of surgeons in Edinburgh, was effected, from the corporation of Barbers ; these two corporations then forming one corporation—It is not so generally known that the reason why Barbers' Poles are striped red and white is this. At the time of which we write and some centuries previous, the Barbers were the leeches, chirugeons or surgeons; and as phlebotomy or blood-letting was greatly practised, they were the licensed practitioners, and their poles were signs to that effect. Originally surgery and shaving were carried on in London and elsewhere by the same person. In 1512 an Act was passed to prevent any besides barbers, practising surgery within the city of London and seven miles round. In 1640 they were united into one corporate body, but then, all persons practising shaving, were forbidden to intermeddle with surgery, except to draw teeth and let blood—hence BARBER-SURGEONS. They became separate companies in 1715.

BORTHWICK CASTLE;

OR

SKETCHES OF SCOTTISH HISTORY.

	Page
CHAPTER I.—Description of Scotland.—The arrival of the Romans under Julius Cæsar.—His Victory on the Kentish Shore.—Descriptions from the Commentaries.— Julius Agricola.— Boadicea.— The Druids.— Story of the Mistletoe: (*Potter's American Monthly.*")	9
CHAPTER II.—St. Ninian, Palladius and St. Columba.—Duncan, King of Scotland.—Macbeth.—Extracts from Shakespeare.—Soliloquy of Macbeth. —Ditto.—Malcolm and Macduff in the English Court.—Macbeth on the death of his Queen.—Malcolm and Macduff after the Battle of Dunsinane.—William the Conqueror.—The Battle of Hastings by Charles Dickens.—Fugitives from England.—Edgar and his sister Margaret.—Malcolm marries Margaret	18
CHAPTER III.—Queen Margaret.—The Tartan.—Antiquity of the Tartan by Hogg the Ettrick Shepherd.—Deaths of Malcolm and Margaret.—David.— Matilda.— Alexander.— Malcolm II.—William the Lion.—Alexander II.—Alexander III.—The Maid of Norway.—Bruce and Baliol.—William Wallace.— His History.— Lament of Wallace, by Thomas Campbell.—The Abbot and Bruce, by Sir Walter Scott.—Romantic Adventures of Bruce.—The Brooch of Lorn, by Sir Walter Scott.—The Blood Hound	32
CHAPTER IV.—Bruce and the Spider.—Taking of Edinburgh Castle by Sir Thomas Randolph.—Battle of Bannockburn.—The Death of De Boune. —"Bruce's Address," by Robert Burns.—Poem on "*The Battle of Bannockburn.*"	60

Page

CHAPTER V.—Raid into England by Douglas.—Death of Robert Bruce.—Lord James Douglas.—Fight with the Moors.—The Heart of Bruce.—Origin of the House of Lockhart and of the Crests of Douglas and Borthwick.—The Legend of the Heart of Bruce, by Lady Flora Hastings............ 73

CHAPTER VI.—The Feudal System.—Lord and Vassal 87

CHAPTER VII.—David II.—Battle of Halidon.—The Knight of Liddesdale.—Robert II.—Otterburn or Chevy Chase.—John or Robert III.—Title of Duke first used.—Another raid into England. — Henry Hotspur. — Extracts from Shakespeare's 1st Part of Henry IV.................. 91

CHAPTER VIII.—James I.—Death of his father.—James taken to England.—Sir William de Borthwick.—Borthwick Castle, and Borthwick Church.—The Earl of Lennox.—Sir Robert Graham.—Death of the King at Perth.—Brave Lady Douglas.—Punishment of the Conspirators, from "Drummond's Scotland" 1861...................... 99

CHAPTER IX.—James II.—His birth.—The Lord of Lorne.—Wars of the Roses.—Death of the "Milk White Dove."—Siege of Roxburgh.—Death of James 105

CHAPTER X.—James III.—The favorite Cochrane.—Sir Andrew Borthwick.—Battle of Sauchie Burn.—The Grey Horse.—Extracts from the Historical Novelist " Grant.".. 108

CHAPTER XI.—James IV.—His Iron Belt.—Bell the Cat.—Kilspindie.—Marriage of James with Margaret Tudor.—"The Thistle and the Rose."—Flodden from Sir Walter Scott.—Borthwick the Commander of Artillery.—Flodden by Mackenzie.—Drummond's Flodden.—" News of Battle," by Aytoun.—" The Flowers of the Forest," by Miss Elliott and Do. by Mrs. Cockburn 118

Page

CHAPTER XII.—James V.—Sir David Lindsay.—The King Escapes.—The House of Douglas.—Solway Frith.—Death of the King at Falkland.—Extracts from the "Lady of the Lake."—Don Roderick and Fitz-James 132

CHAPTER XIII.— Cardinal Beaton.—Wishart.—John Knox.—Death of Wishart and Beaton.—Sir John Borthwick.—The Galleys.—Mary of Guise. Siege of Leith.. 141

CHAPTER XIV.—Queen Mary.—Her Birth.—Stay at Linlithgow.—Coronation.—The Five Marys.—Sent to France.—Arrival.—Life at St. Germain's.—The Convent.—Life in France........................ 145

CHAPTER XV.—Francis II.—The Dauphin.—Interview of Francis and Mary.— Betrothal, —The Marriage-—Miss Benger's Translation of Buchanan's description of Queen Mary........................ 150

CHAPTER XVI.—Description of the Scottish Nation by Buchanan.—Title of Francis and Mary.—Death of Francis. — The Queen's Mourning Seal. — Preparation to return to Scotland. — Leaving France.—Adieu.—Bell's " Mary Queen of Scots." 158

CHAPTER XVII.— Mary's return to Scotland.—Arrival at Leith.—The Queen and her Reception.—Holyrood.—Lord James Stuart.—The Queen at the head of her Army.—The Queen in the Parliament House... 170

CHAPTER XVIII.—Mary's immediate History after her return.—Queen Elizabeth.—Knox.—Marriage of Mary, subject of speculation. — Interview between Mary and Knox................................. 176

CHAPTER XIX.—Murray.—War between Mary and Murray.—Her appearance.—Suitors.—Castlelar. Lord Robert Dudley.—Lord Henry Darnley.—Her Marriage with Darnley. — Rizzio. — Lord Ruthven.—Death of Rizzio.—Birth of James VI. Queen Elizabeth.—Education of the Prince.—Quarrels between Mary and Darnley.—Mary makes a tour to the Borders.............................. 181

CHAPTER XX.—The Queen's Border Ride.—Her fever.—Return to Craigmillar Castle.—Hatching Conspiracy.—Christening of James VI.—Darnley's illness.—Journey to Kirk of Field.—Death of Darnley.. 190

CHAPTER XXI.—Movements of the Queen after the death of Darnley.—Popular Feeling.—Elizabeth's Letter.—Intimacy with Bothwell.—Mock trial of Bothwell.—Acquittal.—Mary's devotion to Bothwell.—Her return to Edinburgh.—Seduction of Mary by Bothwell.—Marriage of Mary and Bothwell... 196

CHAPTER XXII.—Confederacy of Nobles.—The Queen goes to Borthwick Castle.—"Borthwick Castle."—"The House of Borthwick."—Origin and History of the Name and House.—Carberry Hill.—Its results.—Fate of Bothwell.—Return to Edinburgh.—Lochleven Castle.—Escape of Mary.—Battle of Langside.—Queen Mary's Watch.—Her flight to England.—James VI...................... 200

CHAPTER XXIV.—Mary's Captivity.—Poetry.—Burns' Queen Mary.—Poetry.—Execution.—Spanish Armada.—Macauly's poem on the Armada... 214

CHAPTER XXV.—Continuation of the History of Scotland till the Union.—Queen Elizabeth's Death.—James I. reign.—Charles I.—The Protector.—Charles II.—The Last Parliament and Union of Scotland and England... 235

CHAPTER XXVI.—History of the House of Argyll.. 242

FUGITIVE PIECES... 261

APPENDIX.. 271

ERRATA.

Chapter xxiv should be...xxiii
"   xxv   " xxiv
"   xxvi   " xxv